MAKING SENSE OF THE
INSENSIBLE

'I will do without the spaces in between if you can tell me now what it means to be.'

'Cold', Matchbox 20

MAKING SENSE OF THE
INSENSIBLE

The Ten Injustices of Our Life Lessons

Leonie Blackwell

BALBOA.
PRESS

A DIVISION OF HAY HOUSE

Balboa Press books may be ordered through booksellers or by contacting:

Balboa Press
A Division of Hay House
1663 Liberty Drive
Bloomington, IN 47403
www.balboapress.com.au
1-(877) 407-4847

ISBN: 978-1-4525-1083-5 (sc)
ISBN: 978-1-4525-1084-2 (e)

Printed in the United States of America

Balboa Press rev. date: 02/21/2013

In loving memory of my father,
Stuart Keith Murray.

CONTENTS

INTRODUCTION

Injustice as Life Lessons

ARE THERE RECURRING THEMES IN your life that you just don't get? Have you ever wondered why things happen to you, your friends, or your family? Have you tried to put the jigsaw puzzle of your life together, and somehow all the pieces don't quite fit? These are some of the questions we ask, because hardships and setbacks are experienced by us all. They often feel unfair and unjust, rather than like opportunities to grow into our best possible self.

The aim of this book is to provide fresh insight and understanding into these difficult, often painful, and unfair events. Instead of seeing them as a series of random occurrences that buffet, anger, victimise, and overwhelm us, I invite you to embrace them as part of the rich tapestry of your life, as lessons to learn and grow from. We will explore ten injustices that can occur in our childhood or as adults, or that run throughout our life as a recurrent theme. They are often the events of which we spend a lifetime trying to make sense. The lessons of injustice come to us in three ways: how we treat others, how others treat us, and how we treat ourselves. Regardless of the source of the experience, the goal is to embark on the journey of transformation and empowerment.

The approach in this book is a practical explanation of the injustices and what lessons may be learnt. I use real-life examples and information derived from years of hands-on experience, and I am seeking to open your minds to new and exciting perceptions of the meaning and purpose of our lives.

Our Childhood and Our Children

By understanding the impact of our early years, we can identify where patterns have formed. At the same time, we can assess how we are raising our own children and discover what patterns we are creating or repeating now. *The important aspect to remember is that none of us are here to avoid injustice, but to grow and learn through the experiences of injustice.* We will face these lessons at some point and in some way to enable us to grow into our whole selves. The same applies to our children.

Overt and Subtle Lessons

Where overt abuse occurs, we can clearly identify the impact it has on us. Overt abuse is an extreme expression of injustice such as rape, incest, domestic violence, murder, fraud, assault, and so forth. But we can still learn to heal and grow in positive ways when we have experienced overt abuse.

It is the subtle lessons of injustice that become harder for us to identify and others to understand. Humanistic psychology believes that we are here to evolve by drawing in experiences that enable us to know ourselves. This means that experiences become subtle but feel big to us because they are how we are going to learn the lessons of injustice. Subtle events could include having to say no, asserting our needs, and setting healthy boundaries. In subtle lessons we are challenged by the power of perception and interpretation to make sense of our experiences. It is important not to judge or blame our circumstances, but to accept them as they are and to focus on learning the lesson.

The Journey of the Soul

The ego tends to be in control, and so we take from our experiences the negative aspects of an event and spiral downwards, creating more and more injustice for ourselves and others. The opportunity to each and every one of us is to turn that around and see the value of the experience.

The purpose of your lessons is to strip your ego bare and allow your adult self to rebuild you as a whole, unified, and humble human being. In this way our egos becomes aligned with our souls. Our big 'I' and little 'i' are one.

Observation and Experience

I have been a keen observer of life and people since I was a child. My father nurtured this natural ability in my formative years, and he shared his wisdom to assist me in connecting the dots of how current events influence future realities. As I worked with teenagers as a secondary school teacher and in welfare as a youth worker, patterns of injustice began to coalesce. These early observations consolidated themselves in my business as a naturopath, as I worked with adults and children in healing their life experiences. The content in this book reflects the journey of hundreds of people.

My dad used to tell me, 'You only have to make the mistakes that are yours to make and learn from. The rest you can learn from others and avoid making your life too hard. The skill is figuring out which ones are yours to learn and which you can learn from others.' I hope this book helps each of you to find the answer to my dad's guiding words.

How to Use This Book

You don't have to read this book from start to finish; each chapter is self-contained. The final chapter details ways you can practice self-care and integrate daily activities to assist you in processing the insights shared with each injustice description. Ultimately, this is your process, your life adventure, and you have to do it your way. Simply allow the words to take you on a journey into your perceptions, interpretations, and memories because that is the place real healing begins. You cannot heal that which you are not conscious of. The purpose of this book is to assist you in becoming conscious of the lessons within injustice.

The injustices are:

- The Injustice of Idleness
- The Injustice of Hypocrisy
- The Injustice of Deception
- The Injustice of Limitations
- The Injustice of Temptation
- The Injustice of Selfishness
- The Injustice of Vanity
- The Injustice of Intimidation
- The Injustice of Emotionality
- The Injustice of Injustice

CHAPTER 1

The Injustice of Idleness

'I don't think the world has to move around me,
but could you just at least try?'
'Where Is Your Heart?' Kelly Clarkson

THE INJUSTICE OF IDLENESS APPEARS in our lives when we become plagued by issues of indecision, procrastination, and anxiety. These qualities can infiltrate all aspects of our lives and feed each other when we attempt to find the balance between too much and too little in our daily living. The illusive fine line is an individual reality. There are no rules or guidelines that will tell us where to find our personal sense of balance, but there are plenty of people willing to tell us their perspective. Instead, we will have to find our centre of equilibrium and allow it to be different from others.

As we strive for that elusive middle way, we risk making mistakes and wrong decisions. After we experience failure, our underlying desire for the ideal point of equilibrium, that point of perfection, triggers indecision, procrastination, and anxiety, sabotaging our potential. We get stuck. Rather than becoming motivated, we become slothful, inactive, and limited by our fears of not having or being enough. Through this lesson we will learn how our attempts to create our sense of safety and security underpin the lessons within idleness. We will find our centre of gravity as we understand the link between our emotional needs for love, belonging, and acceptance, as well as our willingness to follow our dreams to manifest our destinies.

Family Environment

Exploring and understanding the family environment is essential in comprehending our adult patterns of indecision and procrastination. For many generations, as children we learnt that our needs didn't matter. We may have been overlooked, or we perceived that we did not matter or were invisible in our families compared to someone else. There are many different reasons this may have occurred.

- A sickly or emotionally vulnerable sibling or parent
- A rebellious 'trouble maker' in the family
- A gifted child or parent
- Someone who was special and needed or received additional attention because of what he or she could or couldn't do
- A 'golden child' who appeared to us to be the favourite child and could do no wrong
- A child who the parents provided extra attention to because he or she could become everything the parents didn't

Whether it is through negative behaviour or positive abilities, there will be someone in the family who is identified as the centre of attention. As a result, we never got to feel as special or important as we perceived others to be. The disregarded child interpreted the family's behaviour to mean their needs didn't matter. They internalised this message and now find it difficult to decide if their needs matter to themselves. As a result, they find it problematic to meet their own needs, to make decisions, or to even know the difference between what their needs, wants, and desires are. Depending on the circumstances, they may even confuse their needs and wants. For example, they may only have enough money to pay an electricity bill, yet they spend the money on a new dress. Having electricity in their house is vital to enable them to eat and live, and thus it is a need. The dress is a want and can be brought at a later date, when money is more abundant.

Finding it difficult to meet our own needs creates a personality that tends to be passive, polite, and easygoing—and maybe even timid, afraid, shy, and fearful in the eyes of others. Being like this has its challenges, because others always know we can be relied upon to do what they want. In our minds, this creates further evidence that our needs don't matter, and it continues the pattern of injustice because others do not consider our needs, only theirs. Our passive natures provide tests for us in learning how to assert our own needs.

Often what will happen is that we will swing from being passive to being aggressive, bullying people, and becoming the very person we most dread being. In response, we swing back into our passive behaviours, feeling filled with shame and horror at ourselves and apologising repeatedly to anyone we feel we have offended. Instead of being assertive, we have created a pattern of passive–aggressive behaviour. To be assertive means that we respect the rights and needs of others while knowing our needs and rights are of equal value.

To do this effectively, we need to know and believe that we are worthy and have the right to matter and exist. When we don't really believe this, our actions and words come from desperation rather than strength. We want the other person to make us feel worthy. When we can accept that we matter, that we are enough, just as much as everyone else, then we can learn to express ourselves in moderation. Assertive behaviour can only be assertive when we are coming from a place of acceptance, balance, respect, and compassion.

If we had to constantly surrender to the needs of others as a child, then we tend to consider everyone's needs before our own, or we want to make choices based on what others' desires are for us. We want to please others and, by extension, hope that they may notice and consider our feelings, skills, or talents. Often the decisions we make, the actions we take, and the words we speak are motivated by our need to satisfy those we love. Through this appeasement, we have learnt a way to have a degree of our emotional needs met.

We may not feel as important as we desire, but our anxiety, indecision, and procrastination often make others notice and take care of us. While these interactions stay unconscious, they remain in place. We will not want to become decisive, calm, and self-reliant because then the little attention we do receive may be removed, and we will feel alone. *The lesson of idleness will assist us to become more autonomous and mature in communicating our needs with others, while at the same time considerate of our role in meeting others' needs.* An opportunity to change the dynamics of our relationships occurs as we recognise that those we perceived as 'getting all the attention' were not aware of the sacrifices we made for them.

As we shift our focus from the actions of others, an opportunity to look at ourselves will lead us to acknowledge that we do matter. Occasions will arise for us to change our perceptions of our worthiness to matter; at those moments, we have a choice to stay stuck and continue to insist our perceptions are correct, or we can discover that our loved ones want us to be content. We may even realise that some people are going out of their way to make us happy. In reality others do think we matter, and now we have to allow ourselves to believe this. When we no longer feel as if we come second or have to come first, our ability to be more direct in stating what we want and how we feel will liberate us from our patterns of anxiety, indecision, and procrastination. Once we stop letting others inconvenience us and start to meet our own needs, we will learn how to be grateful for the efforts others make and how to balance the giving and taking in our lives.

Anxiety Forming Coping Mechanisms

If our childhood was chaotic due to violence, alcoholism, abuse, death, inconsistent child raising techniques, or being left to our own devices with no boundaries or guidelines, then we would have felt unsafe, insecure, and abandoned in our environment. As children, we may have responded to this insecurity by taking control of everything around us, or we may have become defenceless and helpless. As we move into our adult years, this intense need to be on guard prevails as anxiety, which can lead to inaction, indecision, and procrastination.

Anxiety produces an emotional pain from which we want to distance ourselves. Freud identified many defences and coping mechanisms that we employ as a way to lessen our anxiety; these can contribute to our inaction or our motivation. A defence mechanism is what we do to try and avoid, deny, or distort our sources of anxiety, and we use them to maintain an image of ourselves with which we are comfortable. Because they operate unconsciously, they provide us with a great challenge—we often can't recognise what we are doing. Below is a list of some defence mechanisms that we may unconsciously employ.

- When we use regression as a defence mechanism, we retreat to an earlier level of development or to earlier, less demanding habits.

- When we use repression as a coping mechanism, we are preventing painful or dangerous thoughts from even entering our consciousness. The experience is held in our unconscious cellular memory, but we are not aware of it in everyday life.

- When we use compensation as a defence mechanism, we try to make up for a real or imagined weakness we think we have by emphasising desirable traits or by excelling in specific areas that others value or that we think will get our needs met.

- When we use denial as a coping mechanism, we are protecting ourselves from an unpleasant reality by simply refusing to believe or accept that it is real or exists. We know what reality is—we just pretend it isn't.

- When we use fantasy as a coping mechanism, we are creating a world of imagination where things are as we wish them to be. In this world our needs are being met, and everything is perfect.

- When we use intellectualisation as a defence mechanism, we are separating the emotions we feel about a hurtful or threatening situation from our thoughts; we only talk and think about a situation in formal or intellectual terms. This is where we give the facts, the explanations of what happened, and why with little or no emotional overlay.

- When we use isolation as a coping mechanism, we are separating contradictory thoughts or feelings into compartments so that there is no conflict created about the situations in which we find ourselves. This allows people or situations to be either good or bad—there is no room for grey. Things are black and white, and they must be kept that way for us to feel like we are in control of life.

- When we use projection as a defence mechanism, we are disowning aspects of ourselves that we don't like by saying they are in another person. We judge and blame others for qualities and behaviours that we have, but we do not recognise them because we want to be worthy of having our needs met.

- When we use rationalisation as a defence mechanism, we are trying to justify our own behaviour by giving reasonable, rational, and yet false reasons for why we have said or done certain things.

- When we use reaction formation as a coping mechanism, we are trying to prevent dangerous impulses from being expressed by exaggerating opposite behaviour. If this is the source of why we are inactive in our lives, then the lesson of the injustice of idleness will pervade our entire lifetime, and we may never wish to grow beyond it.

Where we fear our shadow, our own violent streak, our rage, or our aggression, then we will convert ourselves into passive, submissive people in an attempt to prove we are not like those who hurt us as a child. The possibility that there is a middle ground in which behaviour can be balanced, fair, and just is often not seen because we only experienced the two opposites of passivity and aggression.

Anxiety and Excitement

Anxiety stems from the flight component of the 'fight or flight' response of the adrenal glands. Our fears feed our anxieties, but the physical reactions of fear and excitement are very similar. When we experience a good and exciting event with fear and anxiety, it is due to our confusion in understanding the physical responses expressed. We often associate a sick feeling in our stomachs, a dry mouth, heart racing, and sweaty palms with anxiety or fear. Yet when we are excited, we feel like we have butterflies in our stomachs, have a racing heart, sweaty palms, and a dry mouth. If the situation we are in feels scary, we associate the physical signs as anxiety and fear. If it is exciting or enjoyable, we recognise the body responses as coming from positive emotions. We learn to differentiate between fear and excitement when we are children; if this did not occur, then we may confuse the signs.

This is particularly relevant if we had a chaotic childhood. In this situation the chaos blurred what was exciting, dangerous, or scary. It may have been that events that were meant to be exciting like Christmas, Easter, or even our own birthdays were stressful, and they were times when we felt punished because we didn't receive rewards or a sense of being special. Maybe we had to give up that time to someone else. Maybe we never got the presents we had asked for, and we were repeatedly disappointed by these times that were expected to be exciting. Instead of enjoying them and looking forward to them, we began to dread them. We feared them coming in case they continued to disappoint us and make us feel like we were unimportant and unloved. Here, excitement and fear were swapped, and times that were meant to be happy saw us vomiting and feeling sick because it was too much for our young, sensitive selves to handle.

As adults, needing an event to simply arrive so that the 'pain' is eased may lead to a feeling of tiredness or psychosomatic symptoms that result in bed rest. Those mysterious migraines or the loss of our voice, or that sprain, strain, or break of our limbs just before an important event, may be our way of easing the building anxiety inside our body's. *The lesson of idleness will help us become aware of our patterns of avoidance.*

The first signs of fears and anxieties will show as a withdrawal from events or life through tiredness, illness, indecision, or inaction when any requests are made of us. Watching TV, playing on the computer, desiring sleep for extended periods of time, and comfort eating, drinking, and smoking (legal and illegal) are ways in which we remove ourselves from a source of pressure or anxiety.

Our disorganisation, our lack of order and lateness to events so that we miss parts or avoid making decisions as to where we will sit can be other signs that we are trying to appease our anxiety. Alternatively, our anxiety may lead us to being overly organised, turning up to events super early, and picking where we sit and allowing others to choose whether or not they sit next to us. This awareness will help us be more honest with ourselves and therefore more responsible for our actions and inactions.

Powerlessness

Powerlessness, fear, vulnerability, anger, worthlessness, helplessness, and anxiety can lead to indecisiveness, inaction, resistance, and being stuck. The ingrained message that our needs do not matter creates apathy, and this apathy can be expressed internally through a refusal to take care of ourselves, or externally by not doing things that are required in our daily lives.

When we explore a concept called 'the continuum of empowerment', we discover that the stage before action is powerlessness. It is not that feeling powerless is an inappropriate experience, but rather it is part of our journey towards feeling powerful and decisive. Our challenge is to keep moving and to not become stuck in our powerlessness.

Unfortunately, many will spend their entire lives feeling powerless. Opportunities will present themselves, giving us the chance to step forward out of our inaction and into personal power, yet we may find that we don't have the self-worth, self-love, or self-respect to take care of ourselves, make decisions, take control, and be responsible for our lives. Learning to take care of ourselves means that we become skilled at how to support ourselves, accept our feelings, set healthy and safe boundaries with others, and feed ourselves physically, emotionally, intellectually, and spiritually.

There may even be times in our lives where we want to make a change but question our right to do so, and therefore we remain inactive. We often experience this when someone offers us an opportunity to do something we have always wanted to do. If the offer is taken up, life would be revolutionised, but rather than upset loved ones' routines or lifestyles, we decide that we can't have our dreams—we sacrifice ourselves for others. They have not asked us to do this; our decision to not even discuss this with them and to decide on our own that this is what is best for everyone is *our* choice. In fact, this process occurs to show us that we are so used to not having our needs met that we don't even know how to make decisions to meet our own needs when the opportunity arises.

Another way in which inactivity can play out in our lives is when we don't take action on behalf of another person. This most often occurs in a family setting, between the parents and the children, siblings, or partners. Due to a lifetime of not having needs met, we decide not to act or not allow someone else to experience that which we never got when we were younger. The justification for the inaction is, 'I never got to do that, so why should they?' Such resentment, spitefulness, envy, and jealousy are contributing forces to our intentional inaction.

Peacemaker

The peacemaker stems from the desire to alleviate anxiety. As the peacemaker, other people's needs are prioritised above our own. This is compounded where we learnt that our needs did not matter. Love, self-importance, and self-worth are sought by serving others, by being supportive and present to others, and by being the nice person, the thoughtful one, the reliable one. Often when we can't get our needs met directly, we will find another way—the peacemaker's way. Inherent in the peacemaker's thinking is the idea of inferiority and superiority. If our needs are not met, we feel inferior. Yet if we can be an essential component of another's life by giving up our needs and pleasing them, then we create a feeling of self-worth, self-importance, and a sense of superiority within ourselves.

In our minds, we transform being a martyr into our sense of worth, importance, and superiority. Of course it's not true self-worth, because it is based in a belief system of lack, denial, and competition for needs to be met. The sense that we are better than those who won't meet our needs solidifies our patterns rather than frees us from the limitations created. We wear the peacemaker as a badge of honour. Holding a sacrificial mentality ensures that we feel rewarded for the sacrifices we choose to make for someone else. This is an incredibly heavy and burdensome load to place on ourselves, and it does not help anyone live happily or peacefully.

Sacrificial Mentality

Often we believe that our sacrifices benefit those we love. They don't. Giving in to someone who willingly takes from us without gratitude or giving back doesn't teach them empathy, consideration for others, or moderation. As a parent, role modelling to our children to sacrifice their needs teaches them to be victims to bullies—or worse. It doesn't help them know they are valuable, lovable, and important. They don't grow up learning how to respect themselves or how to take care of themselves.

If we are the child of a parent who sacrificed their needs to others, we will know the pain of watching someone we love and admire be treated with disrespect, be used and belittled, and be unappreciated. Our desire for them to be treated better, to find happiness, and to have the proper recognition we feel they deserve for who they really are alters our relationship with those who take from them. Over time we may lose respect for our parent out of frustration that they refuse to care for and value their own selves. The sacrificial mentality damages relationships.

But there is a limit to everything. Eventually remaining calm and peaceful endlessly will be unsustainable, and we will have outbursts of frustration, anger, and impatience. This can be an outward expression of our underlying anxiety as our excitement builds towards a special event, when trying to complete a task, or when working on a job. We expend so much energy trying to maintain our dignity that when we run out of our ability to control our pain, we implode (collapse, have a mental breakdown, or become seriously ill) or explode (expressing our submerged rage and resentment). Our breaking point will enable us to explore our needs, define them, and set about meeting them so as to ease our patterns of peacemaking, impatience, indecisiveness, procrastination, and inaction.

Being willing to give up our tendency to sacrifice ourselves for others is like learning how to live all over again. Our sacrificial mentality tends to permeate every interaction in our life, and when we change this pattern, we alter our perception, and with it our world. If we don't complete the process of change, we will become more locked into our patterns than we have been previously. We will be stuck, and will look back over our lives and see how we have become more anxious, more helpless, and more indecisive so that our procrastination is all-consuming.

Relationship to a Higher Power

Our connection to and relationship with a higher power—whether it is called God, Buddha, Jesus, Spirit, the Creator, the Goddess, our Soul, or universal energy—will reflect the early relationship we experienced with our parents. As a child, we often interacted with our parents via a variety of techniques. We may have:

- Displayed passive-aggressive behaviours
- Bargained with them
- Made them bribe us
- Been either a good or naughty child
- Been invisible
- Been helpless and hopeless
- Been cooperative
- Been rebellious
- Demanded that they give us everything we want, need, and desire

Maybe we used a number of these methods with our parents according to the circumstances. The behaviours manifested in those interactions with parents will show similar patterns to those we utilise in our spiritual development. There is a correlation between the degree of resentment we felt about our parents' control over us and our beliefs about the control assigned to fate, God, or a higher power in our lives. Through the lesson of idleness, we may discover how our doubts in universal processes and a higher power contributes to our anxieties and fears because of the expectations and limitations we have as we connect with our spiritual selves.

Where the relationship to parents was filled with fear, we would have experienced anxiety, and if we are raised to fear God, the association becomes an obvious one. By extension, we may find all authority figures intimidating—such as teachers, police, doctors, politicians, or judges—and we interact with them as we once did as a child with our parents. To alter this familiar pattern, our sense of self needs to be in equilibrium to enable us to interact with others in productive, moderate, respectful, and balanced ways. As we mature physically, physiologically, cognitively, emotionally, and spiritually, our life experiences can take us to higher and higher versions of self-expression, accessing deeper levels of wisdom, self-awareness, insight, and balanced action from our inner truths.

The choices made and the blueprints formed in our childhoods can direct us into responding to life's challenges from a limited, less developed, immature, and narrow perception of ourselves. These versions that served us as children no longer assist us to function effectively as adults. The more we hold onto old, negative, destructive patterns of thinking and behaviours, the more we sabotage our lives; the more we stay in patterns of indecision, anxiety, fear, and procrastination, the more likely we are attached to our ego. Our ego can only think about itself and what is happening to it, and its needs are child-centric: me, my wants, and my survival. The ego doesn't want to share or to compromise. It seeks to be in control. As adults, when the ego unabatedly takes charge, it convinces us that we are all that matters, and we become demigods in our own minds. The ego is now ensconced as the higher power—which it isn't and can never be.

When we become attached to the idea that we are God, we block our spiritual embodiment and our human experience of connection with others. We may espouse the adage 'We are all one' while living as if we are the only one. Our rejection of an external higher power blocks us from our journey to humility and acceptance, tolerance and concern for others. If we believe that life is all about us and that we are all there is, then our fear of not being safe or protected by our 'tribe' will activate our physiological brain chemistry, resulting in anxiety. We may go on a healing journey to only find that we are just as anxious as (or even more fearful than) when we started.

When we embrace concepts of being responsible for everything in our own lives, we often forget to acknowledge that others are responsible for their parts. The tendency of human nature to swing from one extreme to another is applied to the spiritual journey, and messages become absolutes and intent is submerged in rules of right and wrong. Our lessons become punishments, and our self-critic has a field day tearing us down with whatever belief system we hold dear. In the end, we are not flowing but instead are being contained and blocked, resulting in imbalances in our physical, mental, emotional, and spiritual lives. The reliance on ego then collapses; distress, despair, and depression may follow as necessary emotional precursors for humility, personal growth, and development. We facilitate changes to our outmoded, child-centric blueprints for living and being in the world, and we connect with our inner truth.

The Need–Fear Cycle

No matter who we are, we all share one thing in common: needs. We all have the same basic needs for food, shelter, safety, love, warmth, and security. If they are met, we will feel content, happy, valued, loved, safe, and secure. But when such needs aren't met, fears are ignited. Because we don't like to experience the pain and discomfort of fear and anxiety, our minds demand that a solution be found. What our thoughts find, as an answer, are our needs. We experience a strong yearning, an overwhelming desire to have the need met, and we keep an all-consuming focus on what we want in our lives. We think, 'Why else would I crave this desire so intensely if it wasn't meant to be possible?' The lesson of the injustice of idleness provides us with a new insight into why we feel like we do. *The intensity of our feelings comes from our wish to eliminate our fears, not from the needs themselves.* Needs are an integral part of who we are. When they aren't met, we fear what that says about us. We do not want our fears to be true, and so we seek ways to have our needs fulfilled to prove we are not what we fear.

Let's look at what that means.

1. We have the need to be loved, and when this is not met, we feel abandoned. Our fear of abandonment drives us to find ways to feel loved.
2. We have the need to belong, and when this is not met, we feel alone. Our fear of being alone drives us to find ways to feel like we belong to something or someone.

3. We have the need to be approved of, and when this isn't met, we feel like we are not good enough. Our fear of being inferior, less than, or not good enough drives us to find ways to be approved of by others.

4. We have the need to be accepted, and when this is not met, we feel rejected. Our fear of rejection drives us to find ways to be accepted by others.

5. We have the need to be worthy, and when this is not met, we feel undeserving of having what we want. Our fear that we do not deserve the rewards of life drives us to find ways to prove that we are worthy or deserving of more than we currently have, and ultimately of what we desire.

6. We have the need to feel competent in our skills, choices, and ourselves, and when this is not met, we feel inadequate. Our fear of inadequacy and failure drives us to find ways to feel successful and competent in our daily lives.

7. We have the need to be safe, and when this is not met, we feel violated. Our fear of violation drives us to find ways to ensure our safety and protection.

8. We have the need to matter to someone special, including family, friends, and associates. When this is not met, we feel insignificant. Our fear of insignificance drives us to find ways to feel like we matter, that someone values our existence on earth.

9. We have the need to exist, and when this is not met, we feel unwanted. Our fear that there is something wrong with us drives us to find ways to feel like we have the right to take up space and matter just like everyone else does.

10. We have the need to be supported, and when this is not met, we feel vulnerable and unloved. Our fear of

vulnerability is a powerful drive to find ways to prove to others that they need us and should support and take care of us.

11. We have the need to be nurtured, and when this is not met, we feel like others are withholding their love, care, interest, compassion, and empathy from us. Our fear of being denied drives us to find ways to comfort ourselves so that we can feel nurtured.

12. We have the need to be respected, and when this is not met, we feel like we have not been considered, heard or seen. Our fear of being overlooked drives us to find ways to be noticed, acknowledged, and respected simply because we exist.

13. We have the need to feel secure, and when this is not met, we suffer insecurity. We assume there is not enough of what we need available to take care of us. Our fear of lack will drive us to find ways to create our sense of security through acquiring people and material goods to fill that gap.

14. We have the need to be able to trust people in our lives. When this need is not met, we feel betrayed. Our fear of betrayal drives us to find ways to convince ourselves that those we love are trustworthy, even if they aren't.

15. We have the need to feel important, and when this is not met, we will feel ignored. Our fear of being ignored drives us to find ways to be noticed and validate our importance.

16. We have the need to feel sexually connected to that someone special, and when this is not met, we feel alone. Our fear of disconnection drives us to find ways to bond with someone so that our shared unity is greater than our individual existence.

17. We have the need to feel sensual, and when this is not met, we feel undesirable. Our fear of being undesired by our partner, or to find a partner, drives us to find ways or someone who will fulfil this within us.

18. We have the need to feel whole, and when this is not met, we sense that we are falling apart and even losing our minds. Our fear of disintegration drives us to find ways to maintain our wholeness.

19. We have the need to have a sense of purpose in life, and when this is not met, we feel lost. Our fear that we are meaningless and pointless drives us to find ways to justify our presence on earth.

20. We have the need to be free and independent, and when this is not met, we feel like we are suffocating and under the control of another. Our fear of being trapped drives us to find ways to express our individuality, disentangle ourselves from the enmeshment, and free ourselves from imposed ideas of duty and obligation.

Needs are needs, but our fear of fear itself is the emotional driver, compelling us to search for solutions to fulfil needs with which we identify and framing our perceived reality—which is not reality in or of itself, but the imbedded layers of fear enmeshed with the desire to be fulfilled as a human being. Confusion, pain, anxiety, and fear lie in the over-identification of the ego-self and keep the needs-fear cycle rolling along ad infinitum.

Social Beings

The lesson of idleness is the lesson of being human. We are social beings who need to connect to others, and yet we are individualists that want to exist even if no one else does. We are biologically driven to procreate, and to do this we need another to participate. Everything that happens to us as a result of the actions of others is internalised, and we then treat ourselves the same way. The more we do this to ourselves, the more likely we are to then treat others how we treat ourselves. The cycle of life and the generational patterns are formed and continued. The lessons of injustice are sustained because we continue to criticise and judge ourselves through all the experiences we have had.

As we begin to realise the joy in experiencing a spiritual journey through the physiological processing of the human body, we open the doors of our consciousness to a place of unity with all there is. In the process of accepting that we are not God, we can take responsibility for our daily creations and be accountable for the choices we make. When we embrace the duality of needing to belong and needing to be separate, we can calm our fears and anxieties to find our way in this life journey. It is through the process of self-evolution that we will connect with the true message of self-love, of taking care of ourselves.

Running from What We Want

As we accept that physiologically our brains are wired for self-protection, which is the purpose of fear and anger or the fight-flight response, we will understand how we respond to the pain and the joy of our lives. Whilst it would make no sense to us to run from what we claim to want, the reality of our lives is often very different.

Two fears permeate our minds to push away that which we long for: the fear of lack and the fear of being vulnerable. For many of us, when our needs are met exactly how we require them to be met, we run, sabotage, destroy, name call, distort the experience, or blame the person who has met our needs. The fear of vulnerability creates a mental dialogue that says, 'How dare they meet my needs when I feel unworthy or undeserving of having what I dream of.' Alternatively, we may be faced with the realisation that our fears and anxieties have stemmed from false beliefs about ourselves that were formed to justify why our needs were not met as children. *If we can't embrace our worth, our vulnerability, our beauty, or our essential self as love because we fear we are bad, unworthy, or unlovable, then we have to sabotage what is available to us to prove we are undeserving of having everything for which we long.*

We have to prove to ourselves that we are right about ourselves. Whatever picture we have created about ourselves, our self-concept, determines how we respond to other people and how we treat ourselves. Once we create a picture of our world within ourselves, we have formed our self-perception, which then colours everything we experience and sets up how others will see us as well. If we don't allow others to treat us well, we are teaching them to treat us with disrespect. This creates a negative spiral downwards, because there is no other reality being shown to us except the one we have of ourselves. It proves to us that we are right, and the cycle continues. *The more we believe we are right, the more others will interact with us in negative ways, and the more our view of ourselves is maintained. Being our best possible self is highly challenging.*

Often relationships push our buttons about our worth because they make us feel vulnerable. Our fears of being less than who we wish we could be surface, and to embrace the love available to us in a relationship means we have to step up and accept that we are what we desire. *In order to be all we are, we can't be idle—we have to stand up and take action.* We have to humbly express our skills, our talents, our gifts for the entire world to see, and we have to accept that we will be loved and accepted as we are by those who know us. By coming from this inner strength and resilience, we will manage those who try to pull us down and openly accept constructive criticism.

Transformation

The transformation possible from the lesson of the injustice of idleness will enable us to prioritise our needs and meet them. We will still be protective of others and want their needs to be met, but not at our expense. Neither will we want others to meet our needs at *their* expense. We will begin to take much better care of ourselves and balance work, rest, and play. Becoming aware of the importance of our need for safety, nurturing, worth, recognition, protection, love, approval, and acceptance frees us from doubts and insecurities about who we are. We will have greater clarity about what motivates us and how we can work with our desires, instead of sabotaging or punishing ourselves because we are human with innate needs. We may begin to flow with the rhythm of our lives, feeling calm and peaceful, releasing our anxieties and desire for perfection. Our relationship to a higher power will teach us about humility and gratitude. In the clarity of our awareness, we will begin to make decisions based on the understanding of our needs and drives, and of those to whom we are connected. We will discover our ability to take forthright action that is less egocentric and that is based in integrity, humility, respect, and non-judgement, aligned to the deeper wisdom to which everyone relates.

CHAPTER 2

The Injustice of Hypocrisy

'What I say and what I mean always seem to disagree.'
'Our Song', Matchbox 20

THE PURPOSE OF THE INJUSTICE of hypocrisy is to assist us in identifying the difference between thinking and doing. Just because we think or believe something does not mean that we are actually acting on it—yet often we are convinced that it does. We are being hypocrites each time we remain silent or inactive on our beliefs, values, and morals. Congruency of thoughts and feelings with action means living a life of integrity.

Life at its simplest is a process to comprehend who we really are. Experiencing the opposites of trials and tribulations, successes and celebrations, enables the discovery of the true-self. Initially it's hard to explain *who we are* as we grow up, because it's all we know. What becomes known is *what we are not*. As we experience what we are not, our opposite, we begin to give language to who we are. It's a rudimentary way of self-discovery, but it is the life journey. Through active engagement, forming a self-perception provides the foundation of beliefs we have about our choices, decisions, opinions, attitudes, and the type of person we are.

Fear and Doubt

Shallow interactions lack the depth of connection our hearts and souls seek with others; with a higher power such as God, Allah, Jehovah, or Spirit; and with ourselves. Yet we do not want to risk exposing all of our personality qualities or character traits in case we are rejected, and fear and doubts become the darkness of our soul. We keep parts of ourselves hidden and block honest, open communication, and the possibility of truly loving relationships.

The fear that some aspect of our personality will be unacceptable (implying that we are unlovable) inhibits the sharing of ourselves with others. Until we learn to love and embrace all of the character traits that make up our personality, fear and self-doubt will strangle daily living. Loving ourselves provides the faith and trust that others will also love us. Risking rejection by taking action teaches how we can act on what is our truth. The more we do this, the more congruent our life is.

Moulding the Personality

When we are born, very little about who we are is known to the outside world. Initially, parents and extended family interact with us from who they are and from their expectations and hope of who we might be. As we grow up and begin to express our individuality, family members respond in various ways that mould and sculpt us in how we express ourselves. Based on what we are punished for, we learn what is and isn't acceptable to express or do. These early controls help define what is right and wrong, good and bad, according to the family.

We learn early about judgement, condemnation, and punishment, but we also learn of conformity, acceptance, and belonging. Survival depends on being taken care of by parents and other adults. Displaying personality qualities that are rewarded dominates choices made, but the *unacceptable* qualities remain, seeping out occasionally and forming internal shame and guilt. By trying to distance ourselves from qualities that have been judged, condemned, and punished, we create unconscious beliefs that run as stories influencing behaviour in everyday interactions. It becomes difficult to know what is true to our nature, what is created to maintain connection, love, and belonging; it is hard to find the balance between who we are and appropriate societal, religious, and cultural conditioning.

Vulnerability and Trust

Understanding that children are naturally vulnerable and dependant is vital for making sense of the impact the use or misuse of control and power has on future beliefs and attitudes. Children are totally dependent on parents and other authority figures for protection, trusting in their power and control over their lives, and the lesson of the injustice of hypocrisy occurs when children feel let down. Hypocrisy in adults or authority figures influences children's understanding of acceptable behaviours and role models truth, justice, and fairness to them when they:

- Misuse their power
- Leave the vulnerable unprotected and unsafe
- Live by the motto 'Do as l say, not as l do'

These behaviours make a child feel unsafe and unsure about the outer world. In response, building walls, withdrawing, rebelling, or taking over control become their coping mechanisms. Unconsciously, a choice to trust or mistrust others is made. Doubt in the words of adults and authority figures to carry out their role with respect, honesty, and dignity builds up over time.

Life becomes complicated as the duality of trusting and mistrusting adults occurs. Children need to be protected, fed, safe, and nurtured, and they *have* to trust in the adults to provide for their needs. At the same time there is this sense of not trusting anyone and a desire to be self-reliant and to stop needing others. Torn between these conflicting needs the child 'distances' themselves from those they felt had betrayed, neglected, or abandoned them. What the child really wants is for the adult to realise the impact of what they are doing and stop it. Patterns are formed based on how a child deals with the disappointment in human nature.

Belonging and Protection

When shaping a concept of ourselves, experiences of having needs met or not determine the formation of attitudes, beliefs, and values. Within the lesson of the injustice of hypocrisy, the need to be protected is paramount because it provides a sense of belonging and safety. If we don't feel safe and protected, then we won't take risks. To live with integrity, we have to be prepared to take risks. We have to stand up for what we believe in.

By identifying the levels of protection in our lives and who provides the protection, we compare the similarities and differences between our childhood and adult experiences. The presence or absence of people who will protect us mentally, emotionally, physically, sexually, and spiritually reflects our capacity to:

- Allow people into our world who will protect and nurture us
- Protect ourselves

If we fail to create healthy, protective relationships with others and to create respectful and self-protective techniques, then we may find ourselves locked into a child's patterns of immature protection by being emotionally dependent, needy, and clingy, or by maintaining chaotic and dangerous life patterns. Forming the foundations of healthy, mature, and sensible risk taking is the ability to learn how to feel safe and protected, because it builds the ground work for acting on our values and beliefs for us as well as others.

Aligning with the Underdog

Sometimes it is easier to align ourselves with the underdog and act to protect others. By being loyal to causes that support those less well off than ourselves, we are suspicious of the motives of others in case they aim to exploit the vulnerability in the disadvantaged. We feel it is important to be seen to protect others to prove that we are not like those who abandoned us, and we access great courage to act on another's behalf.

This does not mean we are acting in protective ways towards ourselves. Making excuses about what we accept and justifying how others treat us by claiming our ability to protect others proves our integrity is an act of self-deception. We must be able to protect ourselves equally to how we protect others, for us to live with integrity and for our thoughts and feelings to be congruent with our actions.

How We Protect Ourselves

If trust, faith, and belief in others' goodness is damaged or distorted, then the capacity to protect ourselves tends to be reactionary. This self-protective mechanism is best described as being like an echidna. In response to perceived danger, we will metaphorically roll up into a ball and protect our core self, sticking out our thorns and spikes to ward off others. The frequency with which we do this will be proportional to the perceived threat. Its purpose is to enable us to disentangle ourselves from others' behaviour and to establish personal boundaries, but this mechanism is expressed with a lot of anger, defensiveness, and hostility.

Ultimately the aim is to discover how to protect ourselves from a strong inner core that radiates out into the world. From this surety we have intact boundaries that hold strong even in the face of challenges that previously found us crumbling. As we learn to protect ourselves from a place of inner strength, our perceptions of danger, threats, and intimidation will shift. Knowing we can survive our sense of security in the world frees us to take risks and further explore the truth of who we are.

Dealing with Others' Hypocrisy

Living with integrity will constantly be challenged by those who don't. The lesson of the injustice of hypocrisy blends with the injustice of idleness for the child who has been overlooked and unprotected when they experience these challenges as threats. Accessing our own fears, anger, frustration, and intolerance of others' hypocrisy brings forth the lessons of the injustice of intimidation. Understanding the patterns associated with allowing others to treat us as if we do not matter or exist and realising how this limits us engages lessons of the injustice of limitations. As we connect to our inner knowing that we are congruent in acting from our hearts and minds, we will understand that the projections we experience from others are merely statements about them and not us. Finding the inner strength to move beyond fears and acknowledge the truth of who we are liberates us from the negative spiral of injustice in our lives.

The Collective Story about Emotions

Over forty years ago, it was very common to raise girls to be nice and to teach boys to not cry. For the girl, being nice meant she wasn't allowed to express anger; girls were generally allowed to cry. For boys, they were only allowed to express anger and aggression, but not their gentle, sensitive feelings. What children learnt was to express the emotions that they were allowed to and that didn't result in them being punished. Any emotion that wasn't *allowed* to be expressed either got channelled into acceptable emotions or was suppressed and denied.

This resulted in generations of women learning to cry when they were actually angry and then having difficulty acknowledging when they were really irritated, annoyed, or angry. Women were not allowed to access and utilise the *fight component* of the body's innate protective mechanism—they were conditioned to becoming powerless. It meant they lacked the mental power to protect themselves or to stop inappropriate and dangerous behaviour, because they had to remain polite and lady-like at all times.

It also created generations of men who couldn't cry and therefore channelled their sad, gentle, and vulnerable emotions into aggression and anger. By suppressing and denying their vulnerability, men have been conditioned to *not feel*. Weakness and fear were channelled into the need to fight everything and everyone. Preferring not to think too much, men were conditioned to react first and deal with the consequences later.

For children, it is natural for them to feel emotions, to sense the unspoken intuitive energy, and to give language to how they feel about the things happening to them. Yet adults tell them not to feel, stating that what they are saying they feel isn't true or real. Adults punish them for feeling, naming, or acting on their feelings and sensing. This creates confusion in children because they learn not to trust their emotions and intuition; they won't know how to respond to experiences appropriately. Building self-doubt and mistrust in children makes their emotions and sensing feel uncontrollable, overwhelming, and something to be avoided or disowned. This is how they develop their shadow self, and the injustice of deception skulks into the lessons of the injustice of hypocrisy.

Even if children try to repress and deny their emotions, feelings, and intuition, they live on. Where a quality is a part of their nature, it will leak out and find an expression. Renaming experiences and emotions so that they are accepted by those they love doesn't change the reality of what the child knows, senses, and feels. It is very hard to live a life of integrity, honouring our word when emotional language is distorted. Through the lesson of the injustice of hypocrisy, we come to remember that every emotion is acceptable—it is what we *do* with that emotion that has consequences. Emotions guide and inform us regarding how closely we are living true to our soul's purpose. They provide us with all we need to make sense of how we personally experience our lives. Well-managed, integrated, and assimilated emotions, feelings, and intuition support us to live a life of integrity.

The other challenge with this emotional-social education of feelings, emotions, and intuition is that we learn to condemn certain behaviours, beliefs, and emotional expressions in others. In order to be accepted within families, peer groups, and social settings, we join others in judging and condemning people identified as not acceptable. The cultural and societal conditioning defines what is judged and condemned.

- How a person looks
- What someone wears
- Nationality
- Religion
- Cultural habits and customs
- Gender
- Skin colour
- The suburb lived in
- The political party supported
- The favourite football team

By joining in, we have a sense of belonging that bolsters a sense of self-worth. These are powerful needs being met, but it doesn't mean that we are living with integrity. In fact, it is highly likely that we are being hypocrites. The human element within us all, means that we have moments, phases, and experiences that result in not acting according to our beliefs, values, or declarations of intent. Hence societal sayings like 'The pot that calls the kettle black', 'People who live in glass houses shouldn't throw stones', and 'You can see a mote in another's eye, but you cannot see a beam in your own' are of great relevance to this vital lesson in life. Each saying shares a similar message: the one who judges others has the same, if not bigger, faults that can be judged. No one has all the answers, and no one is perfect. Self-acceptance, warts and all, usually leads to the acceptance of others, warts and all.

Double the Focus

The lesson of the injustice of hypocrisy assists us to honour our word, intentions, and commitments. Often declarations and longing for experiences of love, success, achievement, and dreams are not manifested because of our inability to manage the perceived pressure when opportunity knocks. When someone else wants or expects the same as us, we feel pressured instead of supported. This doubled focus is like turning up the gas on a pressure cooker: the heat increases until it bursts. The release valve is for us to opt out on the want, need, desire, or expectation. By finding reasons and excuses why it wasn't really a good idea, we distort reality to justify our failure to succeed at work, hobbies, or sports, and we run away from a perfectly happy relationship or situation. We are not being true to ourselves when we do this; we are creating injustice for ourselves and others by being hypocrites.

Transformation

The transformation possible from the lesson of the injustice of hypocrisy will assist us to connect with our sense of joy, faith, optimism, and passion in the world. From a sense of self-acceptance, we will accept and enjoy others for who they are. By feeling contented, peaceful, and serene about life and the opportunities available, we will be liberated from the conditioning of conformity. When we are filled with the joy of what exists, we are happy to simply *be*. We won't need to have it all right now, and we enjoy what is, knowing that more is coming. By letting go of the need to compare ourselves with others and then judge and condemn for the purpose of making ourselves feel better, we will become congruent in thought and deed. Our presence may even challenge those who are not living true to their values, beliefs, and morals. Our light will shine and be an inspiration for others to find their sense of peace and harmony through integrity.

CHAPTER 3

The Injustice of Deception

'Your resistance to a mirror I hear
screaming from your body.'
'Straitjacket', Alanis Morissette

THE INJUSTICE OF DECEPTION LIES in its denial, not in its existence. We are all tainted by this lesson because there is a time and place for deception. Our cultural and family conditioning ideally teaches us when and how it is appropriate to behave, speak, think, and interact with others. As parents we try and teach our children to tell the truth and be honest, and yet this is impractical because we are the first to teach them to lie, deceive, and pretend. Our capacity to embrace the less than desirable aspects of our personalities and actions in life introduces us to our relationship to our shadow self.

It is in the degrees of deception that we find ourselves, because it is not always wise or safe to tell the absolute truth as we perceive it, all the time. There are two biological realities. The first is that our truth is influenced by our perception of events, and therefore it may not be the same as others. The second is that our drive for self-preservation results in our deception, ensuring our survival in certain circumstances. The purpose of the lesson is to assist us to see how deceit, lies, pretence, trickery, and drama create imbalances in our use of energy when we interact with others and within ourselves. Self-deception plagues our society because it is encouraged and rewarded through our institutions, families, ego-selves, and advertising campaigns.

Protections

The complex reality of life is that we are always looking to belong, to be accepted, and to be loved for who we are. Yet so often we feel judged, unaccepted, or simply not good enough by others because of how they interact with us. To lessen our hurt, we put up a barrier to protect ourselves. This barrier can be in the form of:

- Incessant talking
- Anger
- Hostility
- Aloofness
- Neediness
- Withdrawing
- Silence
- Anxiety
- Depression
- Mimicking those we want to be accepted by
- Having no needs, wants or expectations of others
- Letting others decide everything and run our lives for us.

These types of protections tend to emphasize our hurt or pain, and they result in bringing more towards us rather than alleviating our sense of isolation. Confusion occurs because of how others interpret our barriers. Instead of seeing our vulnerability, hurt, and needs, they experience them as judgement, immaturity, disinterest, irresponsibility, snobbery, or superiority. Often this unspoken interaction leads us to not understand why we have difficulty getting along with certain people, but we never bring the misunderstanding out into the light to be honestly discussed. We deceive ourselves that we are not responsible for the tension or difficulties experienced with others, and we justify our behaviour by pointing a finger at the other person. Usually both parties are doing this simultaneously. Communication is vital to dissolve deception, yet it opens us up to our fear of vulnerability, and so we remain silent and defiant in our rightness.

Pretending

In the degrees of deception, where we want to justify our actions, we have to face the fact that pretending is a form of deception. Every time we pretend something that is not true about us, we are being dishonest. People pretend they are happy when they are sad. They pretend they have skills they don't. People pretend to fit in and belong when they feel alien in their environment. Our society rewards pretenders, and sometimes it's even encouraged by many self-help programs: 'Fake it til you can make it.' Not only is this acceptable, but it is desirable; it has a place.

But when wanting to be honest and name our inadequacies as we perceive them, we will often be engulfed in shame and vulnerability. We fear that it will give others power over us because we have often experienced this to be the case. To protect ourselves, we pretend: we cover up who we are in that moment and present an image that is stronger than we really are, more skilled than we really are, funnier than we really are, more social than we really are, or more intelligent than we really are. Self-acceptance of our learning, growth, and skills at any particular time enables us to give up our need to pretend to be something we are not. But to do this safely, we need to live in a society that understands and accepts learning, growing, and changing—and we don't.

Acceptability and Acceptance

It is a lovely concept to think that we can be all of who we are in any given moment, and that in our truth all will be well. But we know that doesn't work in *real* life. When we experience the consequences of being outside the box of acceptability by peers or family, we learn of rejection, expectations, and the pressure to conform to others' desires. The greatest challenge we face in the lesson of the injustice of deception is accepting that it exists and that there is no perfect or right way to be that will make deception disappear.

Once we stop resisting deception's existence, once we stop judging ourselves and others for being deceptive, and once we understand its role in life, then we are free to make choices. We can allow ourselves to see things as they are and to deal with reality. But we must remember that ensuring our survival cannot become our justification for hurting others, violating their rights, being irresponsible, and feeding the world psyche with darkness that festers as violence, brutality, and injustice. It is about balance and working towards creating greater empathy, compassion, and unity for all.

Wolf Callers

The story about the boy who cried wolf is regularly told to children in an attempt to teach them a lesson about lying.

In the lesson of the injustice of deception, the concept that nobody believes a liar even if they are telling the truth is paramount. Initially we may be drawn to people because they seem interesting or different to ourselves, due to the hype and excitement or the mystery and aloofness of their lives. But eventually we tune out on people who embellish or live so chaotically that we think their dramas are self-created. It's not just the imaginary stories that we tune out, either; people who have always done everything we have, but bigger and grander (or more disastrous or painful) than us, become less interesting in time.

Likewise, wanting others to trust and open up to us rather than staying guarded changes how we interact with them. We don't hear their insecurity, fears, or self-doubt because they are shrouded in self-aggrandisement and ego. We don't hear their loneliness and sense of isolation because it is buried in their competition and sense of superiority. We don't sense their fear of vulnerability because it's surrounded in their independence and self-reliance. But even if we do recognise their need to belong and attempt to excuse their lies, they often continue the pattern.

Inversely, if we are the wolf callers, we have to take responsibility for our deception and drama making. We are the only ones who can change. We have to acknowledge our sense of lack, our need to belong, and our attempts to have this need met through lies and deception. We have to become aware that our audience has tuned out; we are the only one enjoying the sound of our voice and the drama in our stories. We think we are popular and outgoing, but if we stop and observe our interactions with others, we will see a very different reality. We will notice how we are left out of events or that when we need help, no one is there. Our fear of being alone is being manifested, and our technique to make this not true isn't working.

We need to be careful that we don't interpret this rejection as other people failing us, and that we don't use it to feed into our sense of superiority and of being better than those who have distanced themselves. Our deceptions are our responsibility, just as the consequences of them are. Learning about the impact we have on others and how we create reactions is an opportunity to develop a mature attitude by accepting the human reality of giving and taking, of reacting and reaction, and of actions and their consequences.

Illusions and Deception

As much as we want our lives to be simple—and we often use deception as a way to trick ourselves that it is—we will come to a stage in life where we can't maintain our illusions. As people name our patterns out loud, we will initially feel greater pain rather than a freeing of our illusions, because we are attached to our self-concepts, our deceptions, our illusions, and the view of the world we have created. It is easier to wear our masks than to face our fears, insecurities, and truths. Yet it is in the process of facing all of who we are that the discovery of our shadow self—and with it our deepest fears about who we are, who we might be, and who we are not occurs.

To become whole, we must plunge into our shadow self to grow and learn our lessons. Although deception has an obvious association with our shadow self, we forget the positive that comes with this journey into our darkness, our fears, and our abyss. It is from the void that all things are created.

There is an old Cherokee Indian legend about the two wolves that is invaluable in our journey towards wholeness. An old Cherokee told his grandson, 'My son, there is a battle between two wolves inside us all. One is Evil. It is anger, envy, jealousy, regret, sorrow, greed, resentment, self-pity, false pride, inferiority, superiority, lies, guilt, and ego. The other is Good. It is joy, peace, love, hope, humility, serenity, kindness, benevolence, empathy, compassion, faith, and truth. The same fight that is going on inside you is also going on inside every other person.'

The boy thought about it, and asked, 'Grandfather, which wolf wins?'

The old man quietly replied, 'The one you feed.'

Trusting Our Intuition

One of the most universal experiences of deception that we create is when our children ask us if we are okay, and it's obvious we're not, but we still we say yes. We are lying and are being deceptive. Sure, we are trying to protect our children from the harshness of the grown-up world, but that's not how they experience it. What happens for them is they start to question themselves and what they are sensing. They begin to question what it looks like to be upset, hurt, angry, and stressed, and what it doesn't look like, sound like, and feel like. Their intuition tells them something is wrong, and their parents tell them that there isn't anything wrong. This conflict creates self-doubt and a disbelief in children. They begin to believe they can't trust their intuition or their feelings. Given the option between believing their parents (because they need to be loved and taken care of) and trusting themselves, children will usually pick their parents' reality over their own. This is how we end up with distorted realities and perceptions about the events that have occurred in our childhoods, and why we misrepresent current experiences.

Hiding the Truth

When parents are overprotective and not honest about their life experiences, it teaches us to hide our feelings. We learn that when things are bad, we don't tell people about it because we want to protect them. This allows secrecy to be fostered and approved of. Young people don't think they can tell their parents things because the parents role model this to them. This doesn't mean parents should tell their kids everything. They are kids; they have a right to be protected from the harshness of an adult world. But they do need their feelings to be validated.

We can tell children that we are upset or angry, that sometimes big people cry just like they do, that our feelings have been hurt, that we have been given some bad news, or that this is our way of sorting things out. While telling children that they are right in picking up on our feelings, we can also let them know that it doesn't change their lives; they are still safe, protected, and loved. We validate what they felt and then reassure them that they are okay and so are we, even if we are expressing emotions.

Until our perception lens is cleared, we will struggle to know what our intuition is, as opposed to the stored memories and perceptions of parents, family, and early childhood influences. Some of our greatest challenges come through deciphering the mixed messages stored in our unconscious memories. When we are exploring how current events in our lives stemmed from those of our childhood, we will find this mismatch of memories. We often have the story as told by the adults at the time, mixed in with our feelings of the event, our intuition, our memories, and the retold story years after the event. We don't know what the truth is, and therefore we don't know how to heal our wounds.

When we are deceived by memories because we try to put our family's version of events into our personal memories, we find they don't agree with each other. Having converted experiences into another meaning other than the one we felt at the time, we discover new perspectives as we peel away the layers. It is essential that during this healing process, we understand how we cognitively process and appreciate our survival techniques.

The Process of Healing

The process of healing involves firstly, intellectually understanding the context of our lives. We need to make sense of the why, how, when, where, and what of our experiences so that we can put it in its place and let it be. It also often involves lots of talking and collecting everyone's perspective in order to enable us to understand the context of the time, place, and event. Most of us stop here because once we understand an event, we feel like it is over; our socialisation reinforces this process. In the Western technological world, we live in an intellectually based society that says once we understand something, we know everything there is to know. This is our science-based world. What we often get instead is mental awareness used to deceive ourselves that we have learnt something. Learnt implies assimilation and absorption, as well as change.

Too often nothing has changed in our behaviours or interactions with others. This means that we haven't learnt from our experiences—we have only understood our experiences.

Because we can articulate the awareness, we trick ourselves and others into thinking we have learnt the lesson, but we have only learnt the lesson when we have emotionally processed how we felt transforming it into a new way of being. We have learnt from an experience when it no longer holds a power over our lives. Until that occurs, we are living the injustice of deception as our life, and we keep repeating the same dysfunctional patterns of behaviour.

The second phase of healing is to emotionally process our experiences. This takes effort and takes time. We live in a society that doesn't teach us how to process or manage our emotions effectively, and so we are confronted with the reality that we mostly live in some level of deception. What this means is that we will be functioning along the continuum of emotional expression. The extremes are crying about everything and being needy, dependent, and unable to cope with any emotional expression from others, to rarely crying, thinking rather than feeling, rationalising, intellectualising, and justifying every thought in our daily interactions.

Quantum physics is showing us it is the emotional interaction with our world that is more powerful in determining what it is we understand; it in fact influences how we make sense of the world around us. If we do not know how to manage the emotional data, we will tend towards deception as our way of coping with daily life.

Self-deception is about people trying to distance themselves from their embarrassment or shame of themselves and their thoughts, feelings, behaviours, actions, and words. When we do this, we tend to use a number of defence mechanisms to distance ourselves from the overwhelm we are feeling. Self-deception as a coping mechanism involves intellectualisation, rationalisation, justification with fantasy, isolation, and projections combined with assumptions and judgements to distance ourselves from how we feel about ourselves. We do this to avoid feeling vulnerable, but as a result we are splitting ourselves off and creating, maintaining, and developing our shadow self. Realistically it is an ego-based process because we can't embrace our humanity.

It is through our inability to process our emotions that the injustice of deception links into the injustice of idleness, emotionality, hypocrisy, and vanity. Our capacity to face ourselves is about our ability to accept our failings, our weaknesses, our mistakes, and our impact on others. This is what the shadow self is all about. We put everything we can't accept about ourselves in the shadow self. The more that is hidden here, the more we have to become self-deceptive to deny what is there and how we really feel about ourselves. The injustice lays in the denial of our whole self; it's because we can't integrate our shame with our humility. But we need to learn to integrate our parts to become whole, to heal, and to learn our lessons. When we do this, our life changes in very real and deep ways.

Our Shadow Self

Carl Jung introduced the term shadow self. In essence, he believed that it is the sum of those aspects of our self that we deny, devalue, and disown. *This means that our shadow is what we insist we are not.* If we are strong mentally and emotionally, we gain recognition and rewards, and we are valued for our strength, then we will not want to show our vulnerabilities to others. This means that our vulnerability lies in our shadow.

If we feel fragile and needy and are dependent on others to be there for us and help us manage our lives, and they do, then this behaviour is rewarded and will be maintained; that will result in our independence, personal power, and self-reliance hiding in our shadow.

Our individual shadow self will consist of a combination of abilities, talents, gifts, and personality qualities that we are in denial of, that we have disowned, and that we have devalued for some reason. It will also contain the part of ourselves we have never experienced because of the choices made for us as children as well as our choices as adults. We may not know all of who we are simply because we can only know the self we are and have experienced.

Our shadow self does not need to be feared; in fact when we embrace it, it may allow us to change in more positive ways than we ever imagined. Through the journey of the injustice of deception, we will come to love our whole selves.

If we think about who we are, what personality qualities we have and like about ourselves, then we often have something to list down. Likewise, we would easily identify qualities that we would never want to be and therefore believe we are not. Everything we believe we are not sits within our consciousness as well. *The more strongly we believe something, the more charge we give to its opposite that lies in our shadow.* If we value ourselves as an honest and responsible person, and if we want others to see and value this about us and get upset when this does not happen, then we have a great deal of charge attached to our sense of honesty and responsibility—but we also have just as much charge attached to making sure we are not seen as dishonest or irresponsible.

Many times we attract to our lives that from which we are to learn our lessons. But sometimes we attract that which we are not, because we are too strongly attached to that which we are. This means that if we are honest and yet we seem to have deceptive and dishonest people in our lives, our lesson in both scenarios lies with our attachment to our judgement of what is acceptable. We bring in dishonest people to prove to ourselves who we are not, and therefore who we are.

Where we have judged a personality quality as an absolute good and bad way to be, we have created our need to have a shadow self. The injustice of deception is about our parts, because few people are 100 per cent deceptive. But neither are people 100 per cent honest or transparent all the time. We share degrees of ourselves and withhold the rest.

Sometimes we have to do this to protect ourselves. It's not good, safe, or wise to share everything about ourselves with everyone in every situation. People who can't respect who we are don't have the right to know more about us. If telling something about ourselves to another will lead to that information being used against us, then our personal information is ours to keep. We have the right to our privacy and dignity.

We are not judging the various levels of deception; they are what they are. In the end, they are often choices we make to enable us to feel safe, happy, and loved. Remember the lesson is not that we do this—it's that we create injustice to ourselves and to the world around us when we deny that we do it. Our need for absolutes, for perfection, for right and wrong, for good and bad, and for light and dark is the lesson. Allowing the positive integration of that which we are with that which we are not is life changing.

Exposing Secrets

Unfortunately we are currently living in a time when the media acts as if there is no such thing as private information, and instead they use it as fodder to sell their magazines or newspapers and increase ratings on their television shows. The most extreme of this is exposed when they justify their actions based on the idea, 'If you are a public figure, then you have *asked* for your secrets to be exposed.' This has included abuse experienced in childhood, rape, miscarriage, adoption, and other painful experiences. When we tune in to the show or buy the magazine, we are participating in the deception and lies, which only encourages them more, fuelling the injustice on all levels.

What must be remembered is that what happened in a context of time, place, and circumstance needs to remain in that context. Who we were at that time, the decisions that we made, and the consequences of our choices have impacted how we have moved forward from that experience. We may be different now and don't want our lives to be tainted by our pasts. We want to be dealt with as we are, not who we were. That which we feel ashamed of now because of who we were back then can feed into our fears and self-doubt, fuelling our shadow self.

Sexual secrets are often a good example of the duality of the shadow self. If we went through a phase where we slept with lots of people but now see this as an act stemming from the circumstances of the person we were back then, and yet we know others will ignore the context of our situation, we will hold within us the shame and fear of others finding out what we did. Our focus is on covering over our shame rather than finding self-forgiveness and compassion for who we were at this time.

When we have children, we will hope they will never make our mistakes, and we lecture them about how they should behave. But when we do this to ourselves and our children, we are feeding into the injustice created by denying the validity of the context of our lives. We are accepting others' judgement on our actions and personalising it by judging ourselves and ignoring the context that was our reality. At the same time, this is the information we should be allowed to keep to ourselves. But if we judge and condemn others for doing the same things we once did while declaring that we'd never be like that, then we are being deceptive.

Sometimes it's hard to know the difference between hypocrisy and deception, because to the outside world they may look the same in some circumstances. Few people have not lived lives untainted by poor choices and actions; neither have we avoided others knowing about these events in our lives. The consequences of those actions may have taught us never to make those mistakes or choices again. We may still carry the shame, humiliation, regret, and remorse about those consequences, so when we blame and condemn others for the same things we have done, we are being hypocritical.

But when we keep our past a secret and judge others for the same things we have done, we are being deceptive. It is our sense of shame that leads us to lash out at others, blaming and condemning them as a way for us to remove ourselves from our own shame. If we want to evoke our right to privacy, then we can't judge others' secrets that are the same as ours. When we do this from a place of denial that we have ever done something silly, thoughtless, or hurtful, we are not only being deceptive to others, but we are self-deceptive.

Self-worth and Deception

The model of the foundation of who we are presents a concept of our sense of self consisting of our self-worth, self-love, self-respect, and self-esteem. We are born worthy. No matter what we experience in life, our essence, our existence, our soul, or our spiritual self is intrinsically worthy; it is innate. Our self-love and self-respect is our emotional self. Our self-esteem is the picture we present to the physical world, and it fluctuates according to the things we do and say as well as how others treat us. The ultimate deception is that our worth is linked to our roles and jobs in life, and by extension how others treat us in these roles and occupations.

Rejection that is so deep that it wounds our sense of self-worth blocks our ability to earn money, embrace pleasure, and manage food, emotions, resources, and possessions in a balanced manner. Attaching money to our worth pulls it into the physical world, where it goes up and down with the judgements, criticisms, and opinions of others as we have our skills, talents, and gifts valued by the outer world. When we move our worth into the physical world, we can become egotistical because we are putting our soul, our state of perfection, into the public arena and saying, 'Look how clever, intelligent, skilled, talented, and gifted I am.' Once we do this, our self-love, self-respect, and self-worth are associated with what we do and how others value us.

The deception is that we are denying our spiritual and emotional selves. If we keep thinking money, rewards, recognition, and acknowledgement will prove we are worthy and valuable, then we keep ourselves stuck in the physical reality. But if we know we are worthy simply because we exist, then our foundation is strong and we are capable of achieving anything. If we come from a place of self-respect and self-love, then we can have a stable level of self-esteem because we'll stop criticising and judging ourselves unnecessarily. The kinder we are to ourselves the more likely we will access our purpose; aligning to the creative flow, and with it the joy of life.

By knowing we are innately worthy, we are not attaching the physical human reality of conditions and requirements to ourselves. This links into our poverty consciousness, because we link money to worth. When we believe there is not enough of everything and associate this with our worth, we believe that we can be unworthy, that it is possible for us to be poor in worth. Through this belief, we will deceive ourselves that our society's perceptions, expectations, and ethos are real, valid, and unquestionable. As we step out of this illusion and deception, we will transform our beliefs and our lives to reflect our wholeness, unity, and connection to the oneness that is our truth.

Mistletoe People

Within the experience of the injustice of deception as a life lesson, some of us will come to face how others experience us. The Johari Window presents a framework that allows us to understand that:

- There is information about ourselves that only we know
- There is information that is shared with others
- There are things about us that others know that we are unaware of
- There will be aspects of our personality that are yet to be experienced or discovered

Based upon this theory, the Johari Window helps explain why our expression of ourselves as mistletoe people will be known by others but unknown to ourselves. We will not treat others poorly consciously, but their experience of us is valid and real. At some point in our lives, we will come to realise that our happiness is hindered by our own personality.

Our coping mechanism as a mistletoe person will need to be released and transformed into a more loving and open acceptance of ourselves and others. As a mistletoe person, we are deceptive; we need others to feed off, and we remain strong while we have people around us to control and manipulate. We leech the energy of others, and the people under our control don't feel like they have any other option than to do what we want. Obedience is highly prized, and our needs and happiness come first while everyone else comes second. If people don't comply with the demands and rules we have set, then we will punish them via silence, verbal abuse, emotional blackmail, tears, or exclusion, ignoring until they toe the line—or we may just lie about them to force them back into line.

We tend to tell whoever will listen just how hard done by we are by our ungrateful and disobedient child, friend, partner, or parent. Our indignation is great! We can only see what someone else has done wrong, and we tend to proclaim our rightness in any situation. We will demand that the absolute ownership of the problem is with others. We will talk about all we have done for those in our lives, and how we are seen as a kind, loving, and nice person by everyone else. We will not see any fault in ourselves. Even when we openly describe what others may tell us is our nasty, less desirable side, we will dismiss it as no big deal; it's our right to act or feel like that, because we have our reasons for doing what we do. We don't take responsibility for our half of anything. The reality is that we are often genuinely considerate to other people. We extrapolate from such behaviour that we are 'nice' to everyone. For the people who are being badly treated, controlled, and trapped by us, they are tricked into believing that at some point, if they could just obey us for long enough, we would be sympathetic to them, too. Due to our lack of awareness, we can't see what we are doing, and consequently we don't own the responsibility for our actions or change these deeply rooted patterns of behaviour.

As mistletoe people we live off others' energies; we need someone to be weak, submissive, and trapped by us so that we can feel strong. Like the mistletoe plant, we suck the life out of that to which we are attached. We are master manipulators and are excessively self-deceptive to maintain these patterns of survival. We use fear and conditional love as our controls. Others are often too scared to disobey us, and because they love us, they don't want to hurt our feelings. Besides, we demand that they prove to us that they love us by doing everything we request of them. We want to know and control everything about those we love. We may even live our life through others, taking the glory for their accomplishments and punishing them for their failures because they have bought us shame. Despite our bravado, we don't feel okay about ourselves. We boost up our egos by putting others down. We collect money, cars, property, possessions, or jewellery to prove we are better than everyone else. We have to be the best in our chosen field or pretend we are, or we steal others' work and call it our own just so that we never have to face our imperfections.

We want to have everything that is seen as desirable by others, and this leads to us needing to outdo our friends, family, and neighbours. This is best known as the 'keeping up with the Joneses' mentality, except we want to be the Joneses and have everyone keeping up with *us*. Our competitive nature can even play out when we make people feel uncomfortable just so that we can steal their energy. We like to keep people on the back foot. We like to have the upper hand, and we like conformity. We like others to feel vulnerable and feed off their fears and insecurity. We believe that others need us, that they need our love, support, and blessing. We are very egocentric and selfish in this way. We are often bullies—yet we will act as if we are the sweetest, most loving people on the planet. We would read this description and know someone like this, and we'd think how terrible they are, never seeing ourselves in the description.

When we live with or know mistletoe people, we have to recognise what motivates them and make our own choices about how we interact with them. Their deep sense of lack and insecurity disguised as arrogance and superiority can only change when they face themselves. We cannot change them. We can do everything they ask, and still they will want more. We can rebel against them, be angry, yell and scream at them all we like, but that doesn't change how they feel about themselves. In fact we may solidify their behaviours because they will feel more unloved than before. With compassion and empathy, we can view them through their weaknesses and love them just the way they are. The most important personal development step we can take is to learn who we are, accept it, and love from our truth. When we do this from our heart centre with safe, respectful boundaries, then we will enjoy the mistletoe people in our lives because we don't need anything from them. We are happy to simply enjoy them, feeling no desire to change or fix them, but we will have to be firm and maintain our boundaries at all times.

Ignorance, Bliss, and Deception

There is an old saying that ignorance is bliss, but ignorance can only be maintained by lies, denial, and deception. It takes a lot of hard work to ignore the truth and remain ill-informed or misinformed. Whatever our ignorance may be, we do it because we want to believe what we want, what suits us, and what maintains our reality. When we do this we seek out, maintain, and create lies. We gather with others to support our lies. The media feeds our lies. We prefer to stay like ostriches with our heads in the sand, because we convince ourselves that it meets our needs.

When we are in the habit of ignoring information, we will often ignore people. The injustice of ignorance is about how we deny others by refusing to acknowledge them as they are. Instead, we blame them for their actions and the impact it has on us. Within the deception is the reality that we focus on the impact others have on us, but we deny the impact we have on others. For this reason, ignorance is only bliss for the unconscious person; it's agonising for those who are left to deal with or feel the impact of the actions taken by those in a state of so-called blissful ignorance. This is a pattern within our evolution. At first there is only us, and then we recognise others and their impact on us, followed by our impact on ourselves and finally our bearing on others.

Ignorance is when we choose not to know what we do know. It's also when we know where empowering information is, but we choose not to access it because we want to pretend that we didn't know any different. It's why ignorance is no excuse in the eyes of the law. But a greater depth of deception comes when we reject that we are choosing to suffer because we don't access the information or help that is available. It is as if we want to be ignorant, but we don't want to be held accountable for it. Our response to being held accountable reflects the depth of self-deception in which we are enmeshed. Often we resort to insulting the person who identifies our delusions and deceptions, in an attempt to throw the other person off by making him or her angry with us. If we can get people to be angry, then we can gain the upper hand because they will get stuck in defending themselves and justifying what they have said and why. They are now playing by our rules and we can baffle them with our unreasonable demands, chaotic rationality, and illogical arguments. We will win when we can make it so difficult for others to communicate with us that they give up and let us remain ignorant and deceptive.

For those who are arrogant, selfish, or jealous types, displaying ignorance manifests as they deny the truth that what they do impacts on everyone around them, not just themselves.

If we are the ones experiencing the effects of others' ignorance, then we feel hurt by their blindness to the impact of their choices; by their deafness to our pleas for compassion, empathy, and love; and by their insensitivity because they lack the ability to feel for others. Ignorance denies truth, justice, fairness, and honesty. It is ignorance that creates injustice because of its very denial of all things outside of itself. Ignorance is a defence mechanism used to protect the facing of unpleasant feelings and realities. Although we may not mean to be unaware in the end, trying to avoid being responsible for ourselves is a form of deception. Ignorance is denial and by extension creates the injustice in deception.

Convenient Love

Through the link between the injustices of deception and selfishness, we will experience convenient love, support, care, interest, value, and acceptance. This is where convenient givers share on their egocentric terms. Therefore we receive their love, support, care, interest in our lives, or sense of importance to others when it suits them, but not when we are feeling at our most vulnerable. The deception is embedded in their inability to recognise what they are doing. As they overlay it with their perceptions of how nice and loving they think they are, they convince themselves that they adequately demonstrate their commitment to us. When we are at the receiving end of convenient love, we feel frustrated, hurt, and rejected by their actions and denial.

Quite often the convenient giver is the convenient taker. They justify their actions in their minds with thoughts like, 'I am doing the person a favour by recognising their skills and using them.' Or, 'I love them and feel safe and secure in their support of me, so why shouldn't I call on them in my hour of need?' By denying the impacts of their behaviours, the ground for resentment is cultivated, and yet when it finally surfaces, they are often horrified to discover how we feel about their demands on our time and energy. If convenient givers and takers immerse themselves in their denial, they lose the opportunity to hear and understand how we have experienced them.

If they become aware of their feelings, a sense of shame makes them feel bad about themselves. This often leads to anxiety because their perception of themselves as caring and loving prevents them from considering the times when they have been selfish, rude, or disrespectful. The lesson of the injustice of deception enables us to learn how to consider others and how we enable others to consider us. The depth of our awareness affects our ability to understand and accept ourselves and others, creating the possibility of change leading to balance, harmony, and respect in our relationships.

Separation and Disconnection

Some of our most painful experiences with others stem from how they create distance. Whether it's beliefs about how to end intimate relationships or dealing with moving away, creating negativity as a way to change the relationship hurts. Common ways of disconnecting from those who have previously been close include:

- Finding fault with the person
- Claiming the person wasn't really important
- Creating a fight about some trivial matter; blowing an innocent situation into something bigger to justify the separation
- Turn some experience into a slight against them
- Manipulating the context from a personal pain, hurt, or trauma into a slur against their personality
- Stop sharing the same depths about their life
- The cultural expectation to hate an ex-partner or only talk about the negative aspects of the relationship, to justify the separation

All this negativity prevents us from putting the relationship in its true perspective. Our interactions with others are left tainted with unhappy memories that support us to avoid connecting with others in the future.

Those who want to celebrate the bond they had with others and keep connections alive when there is physical distance or death do so by taking all the love, connection, beauty, and unity with them. We want to honour what we shared rather than lose it. In the movie *Titanic,* Rose displays how to do this in her relationship with Jack. His belief in her and the love he felt inspired her to be true to her own self and achieve everything she ever dreamt to be. She took this experience and used it to motivate her life. She could have been miserable about losing him; she could have stayed trapped by her life. She could have internalised the loss to justify never being happy again. She could have been angry at many people for creating the circumstances that led her to losing him. But she didn't. She instead chose to stay connected to the love and be encouraged by it.

When this is our way of expressing love and connection, we will feel sad about the lies that are created so that people can justify how they separate from us, especially when we know it doesn't have to be this way. Through this lesson of deception, we will come to accept and value how we connect to others in our lives and express it with confidence. At the same time we will see the choices others make and know that we cannot take it personally.

The Power of Words

The words people use to describe us when we are children are very powerful. We often grow up believing that we are a certain way because of what we are called. When we accept others' perceptions of us and then make them our reality, we become deceptive to our real self because we don't know it exists. At some point we will discover that we are not who or what we have been labelled. Not only will we have to change our self-perceptions, but we will have to deal with how this has impacted upon us. The injustice of limitations blends with deception as we explore how we cope when others tell stories about us. We will be trying to step out of the limitations and at the same time free ourselves of the deceptions as we reinvent ourselves.

Processing our anger and resentment, our hurt and sense of betrayal will motivate us to find our true-self, to dive into our unknown self, and to discover our personal truth. We will have to change how we talk about ourselves—and with it, encourage others to change how they see and talk to us. Challenges may come in the form of other people feeling uncomfortable with our newfound confidence and acceptance of ourselves. As we begin to shine our light, we may discover an increase in the number of putdowns and muck being thrown at us to pull us back to where we were.

We live in a philosophical truth that those in power want to keep that power for themselves. Our personal lives reflect this truth when others restrict our expressions and withhold information and knowledge so that we can't be any different. When we recognise this pattern, we will have to make a choice about what we will do about it. Some will stay stuck in the pattern. Some will try to fight against it but get lost in anger and resentment. Some will become the light bearer for others, leading the way and shining a light for them to transform their lives as well. When we choose the light pathway we select to grow and change. We will question why the negativity of others continues despite our choice for love, compassion, empathy, and service to others.

We must remember that knowledge is power and that when we share knowledge, we are sharing its potency. This means that knowledge and its power can't be kept by those who long to store it just for themselves. Such choices threaten them, and they will try to undermine us to maintain life the way they want. By integrating their shadow into our light, we disperse their control and maintain our truth. This is powerful inner work that manifests as a beacon of light for others to follow.

Moving on to Thriving

When we move from being victims to life experiences to survivors, it feels like we have changed so much and there is nothing more to be achieved. But our belief that this is all we have to do keep us stuck in patterns of self-blame and surviving. There is another stage after surviving. The journey of light and love leads us on from surviving to thriving. When we are ready to let go of surviving and become our best, then we need to make sense of the insensible and clear the collective lies we have absorbed throughout our lives.

To flourish, we need to see what is beyond ourselves and disentangle the societal stories. Here we will see the bigger picture, the cosmic-sized deceptions, and how we have unconsciously believed them and, by doing so, internalised them to play out in our personal lives. At this level the archetypal representations provide greater meaning and purpose to our journey. We can continue to grow into greater expressions of our potential, becoming the infinite possibility that our choices provide. The depth of transformation possible through the lesson of the injustice of deception is profound and unending. The more we embrace our shadow with the world shadow, the grander our potential is to shine our lights brightly for all to see.

For those who are sensitive and seek harmony and cooperation in life, the shadow side will rear up with the suppressed hostility, anger, and hate for that which is opposed. We will be confronted by the winners in the Western, capitalist world who want to avoid their shadow self because it contains their compassion, generosity, and empathy. When we name what we consider to be their selfish, greedy, and dog-eat-dog behaviour, they will react negatively and self-justify their treatment of us. Our experience of this will feel unfair. The injustice sees us growing horns and expressing our wrath at the illogical and unreasonable reactions. We don't get what the problem is because *it was the truth* from our perspective, and we were trying to be helpful.

But others use our concept of the truth to justify how they treat us by saying, 'I was just being honest,' or, 'You should respect me for saying how I see it, because you like honesty!' Their self-deception allows them to deny to themselves the hurt they are creating for us.

The lesson of deception is one of wholeness, the bringing together of that which we are with that which we deny. What we resist persists. It is the denial of our shadow that feeds it and keeps it present in our life lessons. Integrating our shadow dissolves its power and hold over us because we no longer fear the devil inside us; it can no longer hurt us. As we embrace the lies, perspectives can change for everyone.

Using Women's Biology against Them

As times change, we all have different expectations of each other and ourselves. Prior to women's liberation in the 1960s and 1970s, women lived in a state of powerlessness when it came to direct action and change involving their own lives.

Women were shunned from public office or from being CEOs of major corporations. At one stage in history, once a woman was married, she wasn't even allowed to work. Within the family home, she was left to monthly tirades as her way of expressing her unrecognised misery. Unfortunately they were dismissed by her husband and then her children, because 'Mum is just going off because it is that time of the month.' After having exploded, she often felt like the pressure had been released, and she returned to the same patterns and behaviours until the next build-up and explosion occurred.

Regrettably the issues were relevant and therefore persisted. Many women were socialised for hundreds of years—and they still are, as the nurturer and the giver in the family, the workplace, and in society; by extension that their needs don't matter. Each time women believe that it is their hormones that cause their emotional outbursts, and not valid issues in their lives, they are disempowering themselves. Their biology has been used as a lie-creating deception in their relationships.

Relationships and the Collective Lie

Many women have been socialised to believe a man will rescue them from their prisons, or that he will wipe away a traumatic past and make everything okay. Likewise, many men have been programmed to believe that they should 'save' their fair maiden and that they will bring great happiness by just being with a woman. These are societal falsehoods and underlie the deceit smouldering away under many relationships and marriages. The injustice lies in the fact that other people will feel like they have failed or let us down if they don't meet our expectations, desires, or demands; this could happen consciously or unconsciously.

At the same time, we are probably feeling angry with them for letting us down or being a disappointment. These lies of another person making us happy or whole creates the 'angry marriage' when it does not happen. But it also creates deceit because our partner withholds information and their feelings from us out of the fear that he or she is not good enough to be with us and make us happy. Communication dries up when we think it is safer to say nothing or claim to not think about what we are doing in the relationship, than to risk losing the one we love so deeply that we couldn't bear to be without him or her. What we fear becomes our reality when we deny the truth of what we are doing.

Our relationships with others become more complicated as we love, like, and enjoy the person. We unconsciously place many attachments on the other person, worry about their happiness, and begin to see them through our idealistic perceptions. Our ideas about the kind of person they are can include them as the golden child, the problem child, our ideal friend, the adventurer, the family man or woman, the career woman, the bachelor, the spinster, the enchantress, the Casanova, the living saint, and so forth. As we do this, we begin to place limits on the person.

We only want to know and see the qualities that make up the person we think others are or we need them to be. If they don't live up to our expectations, then we take it personally and think we have done something wrong. We have forgotten to see the whole person. Instead, we think they are withholding something from us because they are upset with us. We really believe that our view of them is the correct one. The injustice is that if they try to keep us happy, they feel like a performing circus animal, unable to express themselves openly and honestly because we don't want to hear or see it. We are only interested in what we want from them. We can't see the injustice we are doing to them because we are so focused on our needs.

Likewise, we may discover that *we* are the performing monkeys. Others' deceptions are impacting our ability to interact with the truth of who we are. We may be experiencing the pressure to meet others' desires, demands, and expectations or feeling like we have failed those we love, because we can't be how they want us to be. The lesson for us is to develop a sense of clarity about our life circumstances, to be able to honestly and directly name out loud the deceptions, and to choose to step outside of them, leaving others to deal with their own deceit. The more we try to be what others demand of us, the more deceptive we are being of ourselves because we are denying our true nature.

Where this pattern stems from our relationships with our family, we may find that we continue to attract partners who reflect the parent with whom we have the most intense issues. Our desire to not be like a particular parent often results in us putting these qualities into our shadow. Our fears feed our shadow, and this draws people into our lives to play out that which we are denying. But our personal story of what we are denying is for us to discover. We could be denying that we are like that parent, or denying trusting and believing in ourselves that we are different. Either way, we have to integrate our parent into our wholeness to attract the partner we truly want.

Honesty Gauge

The lesson assists us to evaluate how open and honest we are with people. We may feel we share all we are capable of, but with a new insight, we may see that we are keeping parts of ourselves hidden and are deceiving others in our commitments to them. We may come to understand the reasons we have done this and then choose to act differently. Or we may be honest and explain why we have the boundaries we have, honestly and openly maintaining them.

We can't be totally emotionally honest when consumed by grief, hate, jealousy, doubt, or fear. These emotions colour our heart's honesty gauge. Instead, we do it in degrees. We are only able to be as emotionally honest as we are willing to be vulnerable to our feelings and open to another person. If we aren't willing to be vulnerable at all, then we are being extremely dishonest and deceptive by hiding this reality. The more we are willing to be vulnerable, the less deceptive and more honest we will be. Of course, we can be honest about our unwillingness to be vulnerable, but that creates other realities for us all to face and manage.

Vulnerability leads us to reconnect with aspects of ourselves that we don't want to acknowledge due to the hurt we have experienced in the past. We can't control events or people, and this can create a lot of stress for those that need control in order to feel secure or safe. We all need to feel safe; in fact, it is hard-wired into our brains by the structure known as the amygdala. The lesson is not about safety—it's about the mechanism we use to cover up our vulnerability.

The stronger our sense of self, the more clear and honest we are to ourselves; the more connected we are to our personal power, the less impact others will have on us. We have to own who we are. When we don't accept ourselves and don't think we are good enough, we interact with the world from the perception that we are not worthy. We cover ourselves over with lies, deceit, pretence, and drama to distract others from seeing who we think we really are, and to distance ourselves from our source of shame. This links the lesson of the injustice of temptation with deception, because the more shame we feel, the more we are convinced that we aren't good enough. The more intense and exaggerated the lies, deceit, pretence, and drama, the more we feel bad about what we say and do in our lives, and the cycle of self-deprecation continues.

Proportional response theory suggests that in response to how we feel about ourselves, we will *project* our lies, drama, deceit, and presence out into our daily lives. If we feel completely and utterly worthless, then we will express, in direct proportion, this intensity when we try to hide our shame. Therefore the greater the lies, the greater the drama in our life, and the greater our sense of personal shame will be.

If we are on the receiving end of others' lies, pretending, deceit, or drama, 'proportional response' can help us understand what motivates them. If we look at how strongly people react, then we can see how strongly they feel about us or something in their lives. That means the greater the sabotage or hurt, the greater the fear they feel about losing us or losing something they think we can take away from them. It doesn't have to make sense to us—in fact, often it is the most illogical and unreasonable behaviours that are best explained as being motivated by fear. It is through the lesson of deception that we learn the injustice lies in the degrees of worthiness attached to us by others.

Transformation

The transformation possible from the lesson of the injustice of deception will enable us to lighten our shadow self. We will deal with things with greater honesty and clarity; it will challenge us to face our fear of vulnerability and make a choice about who we really are. Once we face our truth about our fears, we can learn to be more honest about them to others as well as to ourselves. As we disentangle from deception, we will feel light, cheeky, and happy; a more playful and innocent self will greet the world, knowing that we are free to shine our light brightly. When we embrace the need of our soul's journey to expand, we will accept that there is always more we can experience, grow through, and discover. We will stop closing down possibility and potential, and we will begin to respond with, 'This is great, and how amazing the next experience will be.' We will be grateful for what we have, and we'll be open to receive more. Our journey towards unity, wholeness, and oneness will see us asking others to honestly love us, to perform each act with love, to approach every moment with love, to think every thought with love, and to speak every word with love. Love is the transformative key to healing our fears, vulnerabilities, and deceptions. This love can come from others in the form of their support, but it must also come from ourselves if we are to make our personal leap of faith into empowerment, grace, and enlightenment.

CHAPTER 4

The Injustice of Limitations

'She never knew she even had a choice, and
that's what happens when the only voice
she hears is telling her she can't.'
'Stupid Boy', Keith Urban

THE PURPOSE OF THE INJUSTICE of limitations is to assist us to explore all the ways in which we feel limited, restricted, and controlled by social conditioning, others, and ourselves. These limitations come from cultural, religious, family, and personal concepts of an ideal, preferred, or perfect way to think, feel, act, and present who we are to others. The stereotypes projected through the media further compound our experiences of being made to fit into a box, labelled, and contained. While humans tend to value conformity and prefer all things to be simple and predictable, there is an inner voice calling for our authentic self to reign. This duality of desires holds the expectations, archetypes, and ideals of our personal and universal collective chronicles like a memory, which filters everything we experience through our unconscious minds.

Relationships form the training ground from which we can see, hear, feel, and experience how filters are used on personal stories in our daily lives. The key to learning the lessons of the injustice of limitations is found in identifying how we are controlled and limited by these filters, because they create blocks in accessing our true potential. Where we become stuck in the restrictions, we spiral into yearning for a different reality, feeling powerless and a victim to fate, circumstance, and idealistic perfection.

The Idealised Partner

We all grow up forming an idea of the perfect woman and man. This image has been influenced by parents, movies, magazines, and cultural and religious expectations, combined with our personal likes and dislikes. In fact each culture creates a mythical woman and man who don't exist in reality, only in the collective unconscious, yet society feeds our yearning of the unattainable as we search for this ideal in love and relationships. The injustice of limitations is experienced when:

- We try to fit ourselves into this ideal and therefore deny aspects of our true nature
- Someone else imposes the ideal on to us, thus limiting our self-expression
- We demand others to live up to our idealist expectations, ignoring who they really are

Each of the above experiences forms limitations, controls, and restriction on someone.

The first experience of falling in love occurs as a baby with its parents. It is a euphoric love, pure and untainted, that is never forgotten and always sought after later in life. During our early childhood, we are collecting ideas and experiences that form our ideal partner. The emotional image of parents influences our desires for what characteristics we seek. These images can be positive and negative. Flaws and unmet needs serve as stimulus to find a partner like a specific parent, to enable that partner to provide for us in the ways we perceived as not met when a child. These expectations underlie many intimate relationships but can be played out in all close interactions.

Often the complexity found in human connections stems from the reality that both people in a relationship are seeking to have their prized needs met simultaneously. The injustice occurring is the limitations created as each person in a relationship merges the other with their mother if they are a woman, or their father if they are a man, in an attempt to recreate the experience of euphoric love; to fulfil unmet needs; and to make up for the gaps, lack and insufficiency felt inside this person.

Sigmund Freud coined the term 'defence mechanism'. In an attempt to decrease anxiety and lessen a sense of imperfection, the defence mechanism projection occurs when we put either positive or negative feelings, traits, needs, and desires on to another to distance ourselves from our own perceived inadequacies. In these interactions, when one hears words and sees expressions of hurt and pain, love and longing that are not about the person they are projected on to but instead the unresolved desires and needs of the inner child within the one expressing the emotion, it complicates relationships.

Similarly in friendships and with colleagues, projecting personality qualities or needs, desires, and wants on to another and claiming they are theirs places unwanted limits, controls, and restrictions on interactions. This objectification process limits self-expression as we forget who we are when we take on the perceptions of others. By becoming trapped in justifying who we are, what our intentions are, or even why we acted, said, or held a particular opinion, we become an explainer. The more we justify and explain our 'normal' behaviours, the more over-conscious of ourselves we become, altering our self-perceptions and participation in social situations.

Where the projection is the reflection of the mythical and ideal partner, a sense of never being good enough to keep another happy may prevail. In relationships we want our partner to understand who we are, to acknowledge who we are. When this doesn't happen because they are blurring myth, archetype, the idealised parent, and personal expectations of how we should be, it rocks our sense of belonging, which is the goal in forming the relationship. An internal crisis ensues. Through the lesson of the injustice of limitations, a sense of feeling caged and trapped—as if we are screaming on the inside but no one can hear us—is often accessed because we are not seen for our individual and unique self but as a reflection of the desires of those in our lives.

Initially, as we realise that all the adaptations and justifications are pointless or falling on deaf ears, we will withdraw emotionally and/or physically, leaving people to their projections and expectations. But in time, we will acknowledge that withdrawing is not resolving the projections, because no one is being held accountable. By learning to stand true to ourselves, surrendering our need to control how others perceive us and with clear boundaries, we will assert our right to be our authentic self.

Lack and Limitations

The injustice of selfishness feeds into the injustice of limitations because a sense of lack creates restrictions. This pattern manifests where energy is lost, and we feel drained by interactions. A sense of lack means that we feel like what we have is not enough. This leads us to needing more of everything: collecting more possessions, more money, eating more food, and drinking more. But this material collecting still isn't enough. Feeding off the energy of others energises, makes us feel alive; this emotional high hooks us into an addictive cycle where each time we are seeking something that we desire and fear is unattainable, we compensate by drawing in other people to feed off.

Learning to set emotional or energetic boundaries and recognise the triggers helps change vulnerability to the leaching of energy. Draining behaviours include put-downs, constantly seeking compliments, looking for reassurance, being dependent and needy, complaining, being bossy and demanding, dominating conversations, only being interested in the drama of experiences, and so forth. For the person leeching the energy, they become limited by their own actions because they never learn to change their attitudes, be grateful, and see there is enough for them and everyone. Those who are drained end up feeling limited because they have given up part of themselves to another.

Child's Perspective

To understand our fall from perfection and how this forms an unconscious pattern of limitation, we must explore to our childhood perceptions. Our child self sees all adults as safe, all-knowing, and perfect. As a child, our needs are simple. We want to:

- Be lovable
- Be acceptable

- Be important
- Be valuable
- Matter
- Exist

It is from these needs that the child-self interprets its experiences. When an adult acts irresponsibly, the child thinks the adult is saying they are:

- Unlovable
- Unacceptable
- Not important
- Not valuable
- Irrelevant
- Invisible

Unconscious messages are planted that the child is not good enough, or competent enough, somehow faulty, and worthless—maybe even innately bad and born of sin. This makes the child vulnerable to others' opinions, words, and actions, but it also creates the self-critic. A child will begin to judge all their thoughts, feelings, and behaviours from one self-perceived significant event or an accumulation of experiences. The child may form a number of responses:

- They may try to conform and be 'good'
- Rebel and be bad or naughty, becoming the problem child
- Where the adult's messages are inconsistent or chaotic, a child's behaviour may reflect this by also being inconsistent
- Be consistent and then self-punish when they don't achieve the desired result

No matter what the circumstance, the further away from our own inner knowing and personal power, the greater the injustice we are doing to ourselves, because as an adult we will automatically respond to these decisions made as a child with little conscious connection to the original triggers or traumas thus setting up our patterns of limitations, control, and restriction for much of our life.

Conditioning

An opportunity to understand how conditioning moulds perceptions, attitudes, values, and beliefs is an integral part of the lesson of the injustice of limitations. As we evolve through our life journey, we will notice how conditioning influences decisions and choices. The more we desire to become conscious and aware of our choices and beliefs, the more we will be led into questioning what is true to our inner self, what has been given to us, and what we have absorbed from environmental influences. Conditioning comes from a multiple of sources:

- Cultural
- Family
- Religion
- Political
- Socio-economic
- Dominant societal paradigms
- Multi-media such as advertising, magazines, movies
- Patriarchal/matriarchal paradigms
- Feminism

Although we need laws, social mores, and customs (controls and limits) to maintain order and a civil society, conditioning, irrelevant to its source, is a form of control if it *negatively* limits who we are. Where we agree with the beliefs, attitudes, expectations, values, and behaviours of the source of conditioning and experience it as enhancing our self-expression, there are no limitations or injustice created. Instead, we feel aligned to our purpose and inner truth. But where conditioning blocks access to true potential, we experience the injustice in limitations and controls.

As a society we don't want to allow a paedophile, rapist, or murderer to manifest his or her full potential. Those with evil or ill-intent in their hearts are the reason for appropriate laws to be created and enforced. A paedophile ring will form a subculture to support, encourage, and reinforce their values, beliefs, attitudes, and behaviours. Grooming is a form of conditioning or programming used by paedophiles to create easy access to their prey. Within their subculture they breed an acceptance of domination over others, winning over compassion, exploitation over empathy, and an attitude that others should subjugate themselves or be dismissed as irrelevant. The obvious destruction to dignity that comes from being treated this way feeds the experience of the injustice of limitations and the need for fairer and just sentencing for crimes against humanity.

Where positive potential serves the world and feeds the psyche of humanity, conditioning that blocks its expression is the source of injustice that needs to be understood and transformed in our personal lives. The right to be ourselves has with it enormous responsibility. Accepting that responsibility to be our best and acting with respect, humility, compassion, and empathy brings with it challenges from others that engage the lesson of the injustice of limitations. With insight and the keen eye of the observer, we will watch interactions transpire and see how the consequences, responses, and outcomes from each conversation impact everyone involved.

A common example is advice giving. People love to give advice, and despite thinking they are being helpful by telling others how to live their lives and what they should be doing, it doesn't help in the long run. In fact, too often it induces self-doubt, keeping them needing the advice and guidance. Unintentionally, the advice giver has a sense of personal power and validity for being knowledgeable and wise, but it leaves those they advise feeling powerless. Inner knowing can be undermined and can lead to a sense of being cut off from inner guidance. In time, receivers of advice begin to be unfair to their own selves as they internalise this created reality. The external injustice taps into unconscious messages, and they become trapped in a self-fulfilling injustice of self-doubt and insecurity.

Controls are found in the ways people limit, restrict, or block:

- What we say
- How we say it
- What we wear
- How we look
- Our body size
- Our personality
- Our laughter
- Our interests and hobbies
- Our occupation

It's about the fashion police, the political correctness of the generational, cultural, religious, family, and societal conditioning of our era. Each time we feel humiliated because we didn't know, look, say, or do the right thing or the cool thing, or the in-thing, we are experiencing the impact of the lesson of the injustice of limitations.

To define who we are despite these overlays of expectations and conditioning is often challenging. The cultural conditioning dictates that the apple never falls far from the tree, implying that we are just like our parents. Depending on who our family is, this can create limits because we are tainted by the actions, behaviours, attitudes, and values of our family. 'A leopard never changes his spots' is another adage compounding the restrictions on an individual being seen for their unique self, independent of family, peer group, or stereotypes of race, colour, and occupation. In the movie *Sleepless in Seattle,* Tom Hanks's character Sam says to his son Jonah, 'Dating . . . this is what single people do they try other people on and see how they fit.' Conditioning is like that. When it doesn't fit, it creates inner conflict, tension, irritation, and incongruence. By changing internal acceptance of these limitations and accessing self-approval instead of prioritising external programming over personal integrity, we can align ourselves with our truth. We will give up others perceptions and form our own.

Naturally, when conforming to conditioning that does not serve our authentic self, we will feel limited and controlled. Blaming the external source of that control for how we feel denies our responsibility for our own responses. Reaching a stage in personal growth where we no longer wish to conform or blame leads towards a journey to meet the true self. The sojourn can be uncomfortable because we feel our fears of rejection, not belonging, being alone, and feeling wrong and bad. As we access a sense of isolation and sadness, our emotional pain (when allowed to be without judgement, suppression, or rejection) will transmute into a freedom to feel whole and complete in our authenticity. Letting go of the relevant conditioning liberates us from the controls and limits in our lives, and it supports change in how we communicate and interact with others.

Excess

The injustice of limitations is found in our rejection of boundaries, healthy limits, and productive controls as we submerge ourselves into our excesses. We currently live in a world of excess. We consume foods, alcohol, and drugs (legal and illegal) in copious amounts. Our modern Western society is facing an obesity epidemic and a health crisis not seen for generations. For all our wealth and knowledge, we are facing a reality where those born today will have a life span equal to those 150 years ago. Our excesses, our need for things to be easy, and our desire to raise children who don't think of us as parents in the same ways we think about our parents has resulted in children lacking healthy boundaries, common sense, and an awareness of balance.

Each time we face how we are out of control; lacking boundaries; and denying our emotional, mental, or physical limits, we are confronted with our internal, self-fulfilling injustice. The need to 'throw the baby out with the bath water' or to 'cut off our noses despite our faces' are sayings that reflect the human pattern of people not liking an experience, but instead of identifying what specifically they didn't like, they throw out the entire event. This is why society tends to swing from one extreme to another. Injustices are created as we struggle to find the middle ground, the balancing point in our personal lives and as a society in general.

The patriarchal society in which we live is about being competitive: someone is a winner and someone must lose;

everyone and everything is fair game. This mentality allows us to remove ourselves from our responsibility. We justify our behaviour, thoughts, and words with, 'It doesn't hurt to try,' 'Well, they could have stopped me,' 'It didn't hurt them,' and 'They should take it as a compliment.' When we are blamed for what someone else does, it puts the responsibility of that person's actions on to us, and this is unfair. Over time we forget that what others do is their choice, and they are responsible for those choices. The more we don't hold others accountable, the less likely it will be that the injustice will end.

Innate Emotional Responses

There is a strong correlation between our emotions and food; it is learnt between birth and three years of age when we are totally dependent on those around us. Our innate, emotional responses of survival become our automatic patterns for life. How we relate to food is reflected in our responses to sex, money, possessions, power, pleasure, and relationships. Likewise, the beliefs we form about punishment, worth, deserving, excess, and lack stem from our experiences of pleasure in these early years.

Habitual emotional responses often prevent us from moving on in some, if not many, aspects of our life. It is common to want to push or suppress our overwhelming feelings by ignoring, repressing, or projecting them as a way of avoiding our own reality. Misusing food, sex, money, power, pleasure, possessions, and relationships creates limitations on us and those affected by our choices. Abandoning our responsibilities to others, to our community, and to the planet as a whole maintains our ideas that we are powerless and incapable of taking care of that which is ours to protect. We lose what is sacred, and instead we replace our responsibility with dependence and abdicate our personal role in life.

Transformation

The transformation possible from the lesson of the injustice of limitations provides an opportunity to step back and become the observer of our patterns regarding being limited in our ability to be and express ourselves. By understanding why we feel so drained around certain people and from where the source of frustration stems, we will begin to talk about ourselves even if others try to limit us. We put in place healthy boundaries and remain energised when in their company. Instead of being controlled by our fears, we can choose to become more functional, efficient in our use of time, and decisive in our actions as we get on with living our lives.

Desires will no longer control us. By developing the ability to balance the use of food, sex, money, power, and pleasure by ensuring our hearts guide us wisely, we will mature in our relationships to food, resources, and people. Accessing the courage to face our emotional nature and true feelings allows us to eventually be able to accept our personal role in the world, knowing that others have a role to play as well. If we are naturally controlling of desires, we may experience the excesses as we transform our internal limitations that have been created to avoid judgement from the external world into a more honest and loving expression of moderation.

As we take a responsible stand on our personal truth and embrace the balance between rights and responsibilities, we experience a greater sense of our self-worth. We understand the need to hold others accountable for their words, thoughts, and actions, and we will begin to do this ourselves. Becoming aware of how we want to express ourselves in the world free of others insecurities, fears, and limitations—no matter what others think, say, or do—will energise and motivate us.

But we will find the balance of knowing that others must also be able to have a voice and be free to express their truths, even if it is different to ours. We will find a joy in the diversity available when we meet others from loving hearts and not from a judgemental mind. Accessing and using renewable energy for daily living allows us to stop the leeching of our personal power to others. Having a strong, secure, and respectful presence around others will encourage them to share who they are in the safety of unconditional acceptance and tolerance. We will truly understand the complexities of living an honest, responsible, truthful, just, and fair life knowing that we cannot have this without others also experiencing it.

CHAPTER 5

The Injustice of Temptation

'I wanna push you around, I will, I will.
I wanna push you down, I will, I will. I
wanna take you for granted, I will.'

'Push', Matchbox 20

THE PURPOSE OF THE INJUSTICE of temptation is to assist us in understanding, managing, and productively channelling the id aspect of our personality. Shame has been used to control our raw instincts and urges, creating suffering and a sense of humiliation and failure, which leads to the repeating of personal, family, and societal patterns.

The Id

Sigmund Freud provided a structure for understanding the personality. He coined the terms id, ego, and super ego. The lesson of the injustice of temptation occurs where the misuse of id energy causes suffering. The id is an unconscious, biological drive that is self-serving, impulsive, and irrational. It is usually referred to as the pleasure principle, the unbridled desire to seek ways to meet the need for any kind of pleasure irrelevant to the consequences. Freud believed that the id provided the energy for survival, which he associated with sexual desires. An uncontrolled or over-controlled id leads to imbalances at best and chaos, rebellion, and abuse at worst. In an attempt to manage the id, shame has become the norm within many cultures, families, and societies because a patriarchal constructed society is a shame-based system.

Shame

Shame is not a natural emotion; no one is born feeling ashamed. Instead, shame is experienced when we:

- Feel faulty, bad, or worthless when others judge and negatively react to aspects of our personality, appearance, performance, or behaviours
- Internalise social, cultural, religious, and family conditioning that minimises our value or worth
- Inherit generational shame
- Absorb others shame
- Feel a sense of shame because someone we love is unaware of how their behaviours, thoughts, actions, or beliefs are creating injustice or unfairness towards others
- Feel judged by association

Shame is like the mortar between the bricks of the house: it holds the structure together, but little attention is given to the mortar. When exploring the house, we look at the bricks as being the structure. In the same way, we look at the events of our life but not the emotional glue that connects them. Shame is ingrained into our psyches as the unconscious glue.

Shame from Judgement

Shame that stems from others' judgements is designed to limit, create self-doubt, and evoke a sense of embarrassment within. Children are often shamed for those things that cannot change:

- Skin colour and complexion: freckles, paleness, darkness
- Hair colour or type: blonde, red-heads, curls, straightness
- Shape and size of facial features: ears, eyes, nose, teeth
- Overall size and shapes of the body: thinness, solidness, legs, head, short or tall
- Medical accessories: glasses, callipers
- Cosmetic aid: braces

Judgement-induced shame intentionally makes us feel imperfect and different from others. The isolating impact is that we feel as if we are the only ones like this, and somehow that makes us bad and shameful.

A lot of emphasis is placed on shaming the physical body, but the ability to learn and the expression of emotions are also shamed. Examples would include:

- Being labelled as the dumb kid or being told, 'You're not very smart'
- Being asked a question in class, not knowing the answer, and being laughed at
- Girls being called a sook, or a boy being called a girl
- Being told we are too sensitive or hyperemotional, or that we won't amount to anything because of our uncontrolled, emotional expression, from tears to anger

Most have been shamed emotionally, mentally, and physically. Although there is a need for everyone to be realistic about what they can and cannot do, as well as how they look, dress, and appear, it is the addition of the put-down, the sense of shame and humiliation, that turns productive guidance into unproductive judgement.

Shame from Conditioning

Within the Australian culture, for many generations shaming and humiliating children was justified as building character, and it was dismissed as harmless fun for adults. It was accepted and encouraged to avoid children being treated too softly and mollycoddled. Ultimately, this culturally accepted behaviour instilled shame that kept them small and insecure and feeling inferior.

But it doesn't stop with children. Women are shamed merely for being women. Men compete with each other, and the winners shame the losers. Carrying around this sense of shame about who we are has a domino effect. Feeling humiliated about our core self impacts on how comfortable or confident we are. It is evident when we:

- Don't like to stand out from others
- Don't like getting attention for what we have done or said
- Feel afraid of conflict and prefer to remain silent than express an opinion
- Are sensitive to emotional energies
- Are overly aware of how we look, dress, and appear
- Have difficulty forming and maintaining friendships and personal, intimate relationships

There is no aspect of our existence that is not affected by a sense of shame.

Inherited Shame

The lesson will enable us to become aware of the inherited shame that stems from parents and grandparents. Harriet Goldhor Lerner says, 'Children tend to inherit whatever psychological issues parents choose not to attend to.' Further support for inherited shame comes from John Bradshaw in *Family Secrets:* 'When parents withhold and repress their thoughts and feelings, the children have to carry them and act them out or in.' From our earliest moments of life, we will have been submerged in an atmosphere of shame. Because this shame has been there for as long as conscious memory has, we only know ourselves through a sense of shame; this becomes a baseline for experiencing the world.

John Bradshaw suggests that either we pass back the inherited psychological baggage, or we continue to pass it on from one generation to the next. This means that generational shame needs to be worked through and resolved, otherwise we continue to act it out in our daily lives. *Acting in* is where we internalise the lesson of the family shame and self-punish. *Acting out* is where we overtly repeat the family patterns. Examples of inherited shame can be identified through repeating patterns that include:

- Divorce
- Affairs
- Illegitimate children
- Pregnancy causing the need to marry
- Deceitful parentage

- Infertility
- Suicide
- Mental illness
- All forms of abuse
- Alcoholism
- Sexual preference

Many of the sources of shame from previous generations are irrelevant in today's cultural climate. It is often easier for the current generation to look back and see the fears and limitations of parents and grandparents as illogical and irrational. Although we have the ability to resolve what they could not, it is essential that the unresolved issues of shame be released or transformed to stop them being carried forward into the next generation.

Let's explore the following case study of inter-generational sexual abuse. The perpetrator raped his sisters as a young adult, molested his female children, and then molested some of his grandchildren. People within the family knew what this man was doing, but they remained silent. People associated with the family knew what is going on behind closed doors, yet they also remained silent. Within the family silence was maintained due to the secrecy, threats, violence, and shame felt by such actions. The neighbours or friends stayed silent because they didn't want to upset their relationship with the family. Everyone chose to believe the lies told and the illusions created by the paedophile to justify and hide his behaviours.

Once one of the female grandchildren broke the silence, the dynamics of incest was damaged. The reactions of each generation show the way in which illogical thinking maintains abuse. The silence breaker having decided that no one else will be abused, speaks out prior to the birth of the next generation.

She becomes ostracised from the family and accused of lying by the previous generations; the abuse and its effects are minimised. It is seen that it was not necessary to speak out because 'He's not as bad as his father,' 'No one needs to know,' 'He's getting older now, so isn't a risk,' 'It doesn't really hurt the girls,' 'It can't happen to the boys because he isn't gay,' and 'It is okay if it stays in the family.'

The current generation of cousins remain silent because they are controlled by the family conditioning of tolerating the abuse. They accept the silence and shame to protect themselves from being ostracised by the family, and they do not want anyone to know about the family secret because it may taint their lives, so they leave the silence breaker alone and isolated.

Many years later, when the youngest generation, who have been protected from the paedophiles in the family, inquires as to why the whistle blower is ostracised in the family, they interpret it like this: 'She spoke out to protect us from being abused, and they don't like her for it! How dumb is that?' They are protected from the illogical thinking of the abuse, and they don't understand or accept the lies, the irrational and unsound thinking of the generations before them. Instead, they only see a person who is acting to protect them from something no one should experience.

Shame Absorbed from Others

Children naturally pick up on the feelings and emotions of those they love. Sensing the mood of caregivers and other adults is a survival mechanism that influences behaviours, actions, and words spoken during times of stress, tension, and conflict, as well as calm, peaceful, and loving exchanges. Shame can be absorbed and internalised as our own when:

- Someone we love or admire is shamed, humiliated, or made to feel incompetent
- Another person is acting in a manner that, if they were caught doing it, they would feel ashamed of themselves
- An adult feels embarrassed, humiliated, and ashamed of themselves and projects it onto us, requesting that we don't do anything to make them look bad

Shame by Association

A patriarchal society is defined by its

- Violence and violation
- Competitiveness and what is competed for
- Need to have someone who is in control and one who gets controlled
- Domination of and over women, children, and the environment
- Victims' fear and shame, and winners' sense of superiority and arrogance

Depending on which one we are, cultural, religious, and societal conditioning breeds shame about our race, nationality, gender, socio-economic status, religious beliefs, and sexual preference, creating and maintaining stereotypes that confine and taint by association. We feel the shame they are unable to feel because we empathise for those affected by our loved ones, and we perceive that their actions reflect on us. This can occur nationally, where citizens feel ashamed of their leader's actions (e.g., Germans with Hitler).

Traumatic Shame

Some people are aligned to the awareness that there are natural laws and consequences to actions, and a broader context of choice. Having an innate integrity, advanced empathy, and a strong moral code are valuable qualities, but they can also mean a higher vulnerability to traumatic shame—the shame felt about the actions of another person who feels no shame about their choices and actions. Depending on the relationship with the person who feels no shame, the trauma of being connected to one who feels no guilt; has no empathy for others; and displays cold, callous, and cruel tendencies to achieve their own needs at any cost is great.

Traumatic shame leads to the need to make up for the lack of compassion in the other person—a tendency towards perfectionist behaviours and the need to be more righteous than righteous, more honest than honest, more empathic than empathic dominate the personality. Where the person is a relative, there is a tendency to cover up, justify, and rationalise the person's actions. We become a victim to this person because of our embarrassment to admit the truth about their behaviour. What we never do is hold the person accountable. Instead, we take on the responsibility of fixing the impact of the actions, words, and behaviours. This pattern becomes traumatic because we lose sight of reality—and more important, we lose sight of who we truly are. By merging with these perpetrators and believing that we are really a reflection of them, we seek to:

- Save them from themselves
- Love them more, hoping they will recognise what they do
- Prove that they really want to be different; they just don't know it yet

The rationalisations continue to keep everyone locked into this pattern. At some point, by facing who we are and who this other person is, we will give the responsibility of choice and action back to the perpetrator.

Distancing from Shame

While growing up, we try to control feelings of shame, humiliation, and imperfection by mastering skills, abilities, and talents. Socialising with others, working hard, and being successful at something helps remove these unpleasant feelings. The cultural criterion that defines a successful man or woman guides the areas of success pursued. Learning to control impulses and to channel energies into self-mastery has its benefits because we find the balanced expression of the id personality. But it often creates an imbalance because we spend so much time trying to avoid situations that will evoke feelings of shame, humiliation, and imperfection, and our lives become narrow and self-defeating. This is the over-controlled id. The risk is that we become cut off from feelings and dehumanise our daily lives. This enables us to:

- Climb over others in the workplace with no thought of the consequences
- Engage in meaningless sexual encounters and detach from the intimacy available
- Raise children without putting in time, energy, or effort. Instead the computer, television, or video game engages children's minds and provides a structure for living their lives

Becoming numb, unemotional, and devoid of empathy enables the repetition of destructive patterns that crush the spirit of children, disconnecting them from their true-self. Life becomes one of survival and suffering, and the cycle continues on infinitum.

Yet staying connected to the pain and holding on to who we are despite being shamed ensures the ability to feel compassion for others and to deal with experiences with empathy and understanding later in life. This response takes time, effort, and energy to heal the wounds received in childhood.

A Failed Protection System

Shame leads to feelings of self-doubt, insecurity, fear, and anger. Intense experiences of shame in childhood trigger the fight or flight response. The desire to run or fight (fear and anger) to deal with a sense of shame eventually leads to fatigue, both emotionally and physically. Where ongoing or devastating experiences of shaming occur, we move out of the innate protective processes wired into the brain and instead freeze on mental, emotional, and physical levels in response to what is happening. Not being able to think or physically move even when at risk or in danger is called freezing.

Because shame is ingrained into our consciousness, fighting and running from the shame eventually leads to a state of freezing. The child doesn't know what to do and becomes unable to make a decision or say what needs to be said. They disconnect from and stop trusting their intuition, having been told that how or what is perceived is not reliable or true. Yet what is heard from parents or significant adult's leaves them with no options because it doesn't take away the shame, humiliation, and powerlessness.

Because the child is unable to think, their brains become locked into emotional overwhelm. They are unable to access the frontal cortex, where logical thinking is retrieved, and self-protective thoughts are blocked. When we feel unable to do anything about the situations we find ourselves in, we need someone else to protect, look after, and think for us. We become co-dependent, always looking outside ourselves for guidance and support.

Sexuality

The id is the source of the libido, and the lesson of the injustice of temptation is associated with the use and misuse of sexual desire. The continuum of the lesson can be subtle or overt.

- Not understanding what we are giving consent to
- Exposure to sexual information that is not age appropriate
- Setting sexual boundaries
- Being able to say no
- Experiencing the right to control what happens to our bodies
- Consent to sexual intimacy that is given under pressure
- Unwilling exposure to pornography
- Indecent exposure
- No consent being provided, such as is experienced in rape and incest

Sexual abuse is about power and control, not sexual gratification. The lack of control over the abuse and the sense of powerlessness to stop it lead to feeling the full gamut of emotions, from anger to betrayal, disgust to guilt, grief to revenge. But it also damages one's ability to intimately trust and be open towards others. Controlling our sexuality due to the violation experienced can cause the dehumanising of the sexual self and the suppression of the id energy. The aim is to remove the pain experienced when the abuse occurred. Sexual intercourse may become

- A painful and unpleasant experience that is avoided as often as possible
- An ongoing battle to control and maintain power over the other person or the sexual act itself

By disconnecting from the love, passion, and intimacy, we become a sexual performer. When in control, we pick our partners and act as we please, with little thought of the injustice we are maintaining within our sexual self and at the same time are creating for the partner.

Healthy sexual interactions are about opening up to vulnerabilities and being soft and gentle. Sacred intimacy is love being expressed through the sexual union. The balanced use of the id energy enables us to share the deepest passion and connection possible between two people. It builds strength, warmth, vitality, and vigour in intimate relationships and becomes the glue that cements a sense of belonging to another.

Sexual Violation

To fully heal the experience of sexual abuse, it becomes important to understand the thinking of the abuser. It makes no difference whether the perpetrator is a man or a woman; rape and incest are acts inflicted by a person disconnected from moral guidance, societal controls, and an ability to feel how the victim feels. To rape, people must be shut off from their compassion and empathy; they are only thinking about themselves and not the other person's needs. It must be restated that a paedophile or rapist is motivated by power and domination; they want to be in control of another person, specifically sexually overpowering them.

By withdrawing into the mind and being cut off from feelings, sex becomes an action—mechanical, self-centred, and self-satisfying. The perpetrator projects desire onto the victim and illogically justifies to themselves that they are only doing what the person wants. This is not true. If it were, incest and rape would not be surrounded by secrecy, violence, and shame.

Global Violation

The very fabric and structure of a shame-based society makes our greatest fears and horrors about acts against the most vulnerable members of a society come true. For those susceptible to inflicting violation and abuse, the training ground is created by:

- Teaching children to cut off from feelings; dominating and controlling them
- Children running on hysterical, uncontrolled, and raw emotions with no stop button
- Children callously controlling those around them

A patriarchal, capitalist society that does not value, emphasise, or attempt to create balance and moderation but instead pushes for extremes, and judges and competes with any other cultures, societies, or nations that also project such images, is the current modern world. There are societies and cultures that do not live like this, but many of them get invaded through war or economic free trade and are exposed to and taken over by this dominating belief system.

The lesson of the injustice of temptation is found in a world devoid of feelings, principles, and a value system immersed in loving, accepting, and tolerating the human element within us all. As we change this lesson internally, the potential to transform the world psyche becomes a reality. By merging the injustice of vanity with the injustice of temptation, and by discovering the true self that doesn't feel innately shameful and is able to grow positively through humility, we will create a new paradigm.

Transformation

We are all imperfectly perfect and perfectly imperfect. Pia Mellody in *Facing Co-dependence* says that as children, we are naturally vulnerable, imperfect, dependent, immature, and valuable. If we are raised in a balanced, loving, and responsible environment, we will become self-esteeming, functional, respectful, honest, realistic, self-sufficient, and moderate adults. Our innate message of self-control is humility. We understand that we are still worthy even if there are times we act against our own values and principles, and we will comfortably take responsibility for ourselves and say sorry when appropriate. By identifying the illogical beliefs that set up failure, we will trust ourselves more, listen to our moral conscience, believe in our intuition, and define the values that provide good guidance to living a consciously present, caring, loving, and free life.

The transformation possible from the lesson of the injustice of temptation allows us to stand tall and strong in the presence of others. We will feel comfortable and confident in our physical body, mental thoughts, and emotional feelings. Cleansing the shame will lead to a greater sense of freedom and love for who we really are. Life will move from one that is focused on what we deserve and receiving rewards for our efforts through releasing our suffering mentality to one that accepts life as a journey and is willing to embrace each event as it is, free of judgement, condemnation, and punishment. We will realise that we have always existed as we are, but the events in our lives have covered the real self up. Ultimately, healing the injustice of temptation will enable us to connect with each other from a sense of acceptance of the humanity within us all.

CHAPTER 6

The Injustice of Selfishness

'Our hands are full our lives are not.'
'Sleeping at the Wheel', Matchbox 20

THE LESSON IN THE INJUSTICE of selfishness explores a belief in a sense of lack as we understand, accept, and honour our emotional selves. Human existence has not yet reached a point where feelings, attitudes, and beliefs are expressed in a balanced and respectful manner. The fear of lack permeates our perceptions. and the emotional imbalances experienced as a result of this void, define who we are and what we allow in our lives. Feelings and thoughts are energy; our misuse of resources is an externalisation of our internal mismanagement. Western industrial societies focus on materialism, money, greed, achievement, status, symbols, and glamour as statements of an individual's identity. If each of these is a form of creative energy, how we use, or misuse resources reflects back to confirm our own beliefs, attitudes, and feelings about ourselves and life in general. A sense of identity, worth, and validation comes from these externals rather than from a centre grounded in our essential self. The qualities that separate us from the animal kingdom and makes us uniquely human is our ability to think, feel, and express our emotions. Yet we have been raised in a society detached from, devoid of, and scared of feelings. What we experience instead is shaming of emotions, humiliation for our sensitive natures, and denial and suppression of our truth.

A Sense of Lack

When we invest a lot of personal energy into a cherished want, need, or desire that is meaningful and important to us, we are prioritising its fulfilment above other aspects of our lives. If it is not met, then we respond to its absence at a mental and emotional level. Emotional responses vary from a sense of loss, hurt, and betrayal to anger, resentment, bitterness, shame, and guilt. Cognitively we establish a self-perpetuating belief that there is not enough of that which we decide matters to us.

From a detached position, others may say, 'That's life! It's not always possible to get everything we really want, need, or desire.' But when these events occur, and the interpretation made is, 'I miss out,' this creates a cascade effect of fear in the brain. When the emotional security required by our sense of self to feel valued, important, and loved is not met, then anxiety prevails. We feel anxious that further interactions, events, or experiences will confirm that we are not important, valued, or loved. To remove ourselves from the anxiety, we form ideas, attitudes, and beliefs to justify our experience. We try to depersonalise the disappointment by:

- Saying, 'There simply isn't enough of everything for everyone.'

- Declaring, 'I really didn't want, need, or desire what I missed out on.'
- Making a value judgement on the object of our desire, want, or need and asserting that it is bad, evil, or dumb

Or we can personalise our disillusionment by:

- Deciding that we aren't good enough to have what we want, need, or desire
- Believing that we don't deserve what we want, need, or desire

Each response is immersed in a sense of lack. This links the injustice of selfishness with that of the injustice idleness because the anxiety is maintained and compounded by the belief in lack. Once this link is formed, it permeates every aspect of our lives. Anxiety is one physical and emotional response to fear. Each time we fear that there is not enough of what we truly want, we trigger a fear of lack, and we manifest some level of anxiety. The beliefs formed from early childhood experiences of missing out are reiterated and solidified throughout life until we take the opportunity to shift our perceptions.

The various conditioning of each generation underpins the injustice of limitations and triggers the injustice of selfishness as a deep sense of lack infiltrates our minds with lies and myths about who we are meant to be, what we are meant to have, and what is meant to make us happy. The fear that there is not enough to validate us dominates our perceptions. When we internalise this external opinion, we begin to believe that we can never be enough by just being ourselves, and that if our heartfelt wants, needs, and desires are not valid, then we are invalid.

We look to external models to portray acceptable cultural, religious, family, media, and societal images of an unachievable idealised self, which feeds fears of not having or being enough to feel successful, safe, secure, and worthy. Happiness evades us because there is always more to have and be. The cycle continues until we question the logic of all this striving to meet standards that we did not select ourselves. As we realise our identity does not lie in these externals but in the inner journey of self-discovery, we grasp how lessons of injustice come to help us understand and experience the true self and that which brings us self-validation and happiness.

Until we reach this level of awareness, feeling limited maintains a belief in lack. The more we are entangled in the rules of a generation, the more serious, burdened, and obligated that life feels. Wanting to have our fair share draws us into the competitive nature of a capitalist society, which is based on the belief in a 'less than, more than' system. Comparing and competing for the available resources at any cost means we never have to question the morality of our methods and their impact on others, the environment, global consciousness, and ourselves. We may not be happy, but at least we are trying to be, by being like everyone else or having the same as others of our generation. A sense of security is created, if only temporarily.

The very structure of our modern society creates and maintains an imbalance of resources, and with it we reflect this emotionally in how we manage and express our emotional selves. A belief in scarcity or a belief in abundance creates with it emotional reactions to those with a lack of resources physically, mentally, psychologically, and emotionally, just as much as it creates reactions to those who are abundant in all these areas of life.

The lessons of idleness and limitations merge with the injustice of selfishness as we form beliefs about what we deserve and are owed. Beliefs could include:

- Poverty consciousness: not wanting to be aligned with things we think are bad or misused such as money, manipulations, control, and power
- Self-deprivation: the denying of our own needs distances us from the ills of society
- We don't want to do the work or put in the effort to have what someone else has, yet we still want what they have
- We should get what we want without doing anything for it
- We look to be treated as if we are so special that everything we want will be given to us simply because we exist

We live in a world where we have to *do* something with our existence. Life is about the efforts we make. A meaningful life is one that involves work, effort, passion, and drive. It's like we have taken the philosophical statement from Rene Descartes, 'I think; therefore I am,' literally and transformed it to, 'Because I know I exist, I have done enough.' Spiritually or energetically this may be true, but human life takes much more than existing to have meaning or purpose.

Selfish and Altruistic

The lesson of the injustice of selfishness appears and reappears consistently throughout our lives as we reach deeper and greater understanding of ourselves through our interactions with the outer world and our inner selves. We may spend many years healing through what has been damaged or broken, but in our sense of self reaching, the point of moving on to success and manifestation of our dreams brings with it equal amounts of healing and growth.

Our fear of success—and therefore our need to change our perception of ourselves in the context of our culture, family, or society—is confronting. At this point we have a decision to make: either we embrace it, and move forward, or we sabotage it and remain the same. Working through feeling selfish to achieve dreams, to think about our own needs and wanting them met, and to take up space and assert our right to be takes us into the journey of the meaning of language. Learning the difference between truly selfish behaviour and self-respect is an essential aspect of this lesson.

The opposite of selfish is altruistic, selfless, or self-sacrificing. We are not here to live in opposites despite a world filled with either/or options. We are meant to find the middle ground of balanced boundaries through respect and love. A great challenge in our lives is to be able to see ourselves as others see us, without losing ourselves into ego and selfishness or worthlessness, helplessness, and hopelessness. What makes this so challenging is a Western society that avoids celebrating who we are, giving compliments, being grateful, and expressing balance and harmony for the ordinary person living a life of simple connection to those whom they love.

There have been cultures that role model how to live in harmony. At the time when Australia was invaded, the original inhabitants, the Australian Aborigine, was viewed as 'simple' and 'unevolved' because they hadn't built permanent houses and roamed around their tribal land. Their spirituality was seen as non-existent or demonic. Yet they knew of:

- Harmony
- Balance

- Egalitarian principles
- Respect
- Boundaries
- Cooperation

These ideas need to be celebrated and integrated into our modern world, and that is why many are turning to old philosophies to overcome a sense of lack. But we need to do more. We need to honour original inhabitants in our own countries by accepting, celebrating, acknowledging, and maintaining all that is beautiful about their culture.

Denying Others

The more we deny others, the more they will deny us. The more we deny ourselves, the more we will deny others. This is the way of lack, the injustice inherent in our modern living. It is how we create injustice within how we treat others, and it is why we justify our behaviours towards others because we are doing it to ourselves at the same time. It is a trap, and as such we feel trapped by ourselves and the limitations created by others playing out this destructive cycle of lack. The more rigid this cycle, the more we will hold on tightly to aspects of ourselves and fight against any attempts to change ourselves. This disproportionate attachment to our identity, behaviours, beliefs, attitudes, or actions is often experienced by others as us being self-centred or selfish. Rarely at these times are processes established that cater for our ways or needs as well as the rules of our family, religion, culture, or society. Instead they feed into the self-sabotage we are doing to ourselves and our interpretation that it is they who are insensitive, selfish, arrogant, and acting superior to us. The injustice grows as the rigidity of the patterns continues. Hence, the more we deny others, the more they will deny us. The more we deny ourselves, the more we will deny others.

The most extreme expression of this pattern of injustice can be found in organisations such as the Ku Klux Klan, white supremacists, skinheads, Nazi groups, jihads, and anti-Semitic groups, but ultimately all '-isms' are destructive and based around three fears:

- Lack
- Difference
- Inferiority

When we hold these fears as truths, we deny the humanity, dignity, and oneness of existence. Having hatred in our hearts makes us judge and blame because it blocks us from seeing love and beauty. Being locked into fear and lack colours our ability to see others' gentleness, because we are too busy dismissing who they are and blaming them for what happens to them. The more this occurs, the more we distance ourselves from feelings of (and belief in) compassion, empathy, acceptance, unity, and connectedness. At the same time, watching this prejudice and abuse isolates the receivers and the observers. As much as people are drawn to all that is embracing and loving in a minority group, they would never want to be victimised in these ways; instead, they align themselves with those viewed with all the power and control. In this way the patterns of lack and fear are maintained.

Yet others find their truth and step out of this injustice cycle by focusing on people's hearts and intent—not colour, religion, gender, or other labels of difference. They align to that which is harmonious to all there is.

Abundance and Others' Reactions

When we believe in abundance and openly share resources and the emotional self with others, there is a great challenge to be faced while living in a society of lack and a greed-based society. Through this journey we will begin to identify the sources of shame and humiliation that have been infused into us since childhood due to others' fear of lack. Being able to identify the lies, distortions, and denial underlying family and societal behaviours and interactions with us will help us understand our anger, frustration, hurt, pain, and sadness at the stuck-ness and unreasonableness of the fears, insecurities, and self-obsession that are rampant in society in general and (specifically in those we love). The inner journey of the injustice of selfishness is experienced as we battle with our frustrations and intolerances of those who continue to function from their selfishness. Our need to withdraw and isolate ourselves from these experiences may become more apparent, but it still will not change the patterns. Eventually we will move from our anger and own blaming and shaming process because we recognise that thinking they are stupid for what they do only traps them in their patterns. Our negativity joins their negativity and solidifies our reactions and responses to each other.

The dynamics of life and emotions provide dualistic and complicated lessons. When we love others, we tend to attach all our hopes and dreams onto them. If they are trapped by lack, merging with them by wanting them to learn the errors of their way through love creates this push-pull attachment. This sets the parameters of the relationship and maintains a constant tension between those involved. This pattern will not change until someone recognises what is happening. Often we believe the other people have created the situation, but while we participate in it, we are equally responsible for the state of the relationship.

Where there is no compromise in the relationship, nothing will change, and each person will want it all their way and never the other. Again we see the lack of balance prevalent in society, playing out in personal relationships stemming from our inner reality. For those coming from optimism and abundance, the drive stems from their frustrations that others' attitudes deny the truth that we are all one. Life feels heavy when we are trapped in the limitations of selfishness. It is possible for oneness and gratitude to free us from these limitations, but only when we do it from a place grounded in our centeredness. When we let others be because we are comfortable with our own beingness, then we step out of the competition of making everyone like us. The journey of self-mastery often takes a long time because our society is so submerged in selfishness and lack.

Denying Emotions

The injustice of denying our emotions is that we spend our lives living without thinking or thinking without living; this act creates the appearance of selfishness to the outer world and manifests as an inner experience of over-concern with ourselves. The lesson of balancing our thinking with living or actions leads us through multiple layers of patterns, forever evolving into deeper and deeper understandings of what it means to live our lives as the truest reflection of our inner nature. As we can keep ourselves busy processing the emotional interpretations of the events, we question whether or not we are getting anywhere. What does it all mean? What is the point to our lives and to the events that occur within them? What is the purpose of life in general, and specifically our lives? When

95-98 per cent of what we experience in a day is influenced by all the experiences we have had in our past, making sense of the insensible matters to us; until we do, we may live a life of never being ready for what is the gift of our existence. Instead, we will appear to manifest and maintain the injustice of selfishness for ourselves, our loved ones, and our community.

Individuation Process

Around the age of two, Margaret Mahler identified that the separation-individuation process begins. Jean Piaget's cognitive development theory further describes cognitive changes in the teenage years that allows for greater perceptual separation between a child and its parents. The mid-life crisis around the early forties often consists of a desire to articulate a sense of ourselves not yet expressed. The purpose of this three-part journey is to define who we are, what we think, why we feel like we do, and how we want to express all of this in our daily lives. As frustrating as the individuation process is for others, in reality we are all doing it—and in fact we must do it for our personal development.

It is the role of the family (and then schools, sports, religions, and social groups) to facilitate growing children to become more aware of their actions, behaviours, thoughts, and feelings, resulting in their ability to define who they are. Through this process, we are encouraged to form our own opinions, feel our own feelings, and express our own personalities as separate from those of our parents and friends. A number of unproductive situations may have occurred during this process, where we:

- Did not form a separate identity but instead remained defined by our parents' values, attitudes, and beliefs

- Were encouraged to form set attitudes and opinions at a very young age before we understood what was happening around us, and so we have become rigid, egocentric, and self-focused
- Had no influences on us at all, and so we were left to our own devices; in this way, we have no opinions of our own and go along with the majority

Whatever the circumstances, our ability to give and receive to others and ourselves is reflected in the success of the process of individualisation. Our capacity to be selfish and altruistic directly mirrors our personal development in forming our self-concept. What we learnt through this process of individuation feeds the lesson of the injustice of selfishness because it helps us to see how feelings and mental processes are managed, as well as the impact this has on ourselves and others. As we form a sense of self, we are often confronted by overwhelming feelings of imperfection that tie into the lesson of the injustice of vanity. Our emotions and our ego become enmeshed. To make our ego feel better, we often detach from our feelings, resulting in cutting ourselves off from being able to empathise with anyone else's feelings. We begin to intellectualise feelings rather than connect to them; we lack empathy.

The ability to connect to people stems from our feeling centres and our hearts, but ego replaces feelings with intellectual objectification of others through projections. This means we are not seeing people as they are, but as *we* are. When we do this, we are projecting our feelings onto them. It may not be about them at all; more often than not it is about our own discovery of the self. If we can acknowledge that we are placing the feelings we are uncomfortable with onto others, then we can take responsibility for the injustice we create for them because the impact of this projection or objectification makes them feel like they do not exist and are merely an object of our attention. This is often a great source of pain and confusion when being objectified. When we are doing it to others, we cannot see the dehumanising effect we have.

Connected to Feeling

Having a natural affinity for sensing the emotional well-being of others enables insight and learning about choices made to enmesh with those whom we love. Where our personality character is optimistic, loving, and passionate, expressing and experiencing life with great depth of feeling and emotion occurs with ease. As children, our innocence and connection to those we love flow freely with no conditions. When children feel the emotional pain and hurt, fears and stresses, and insecurities and worries of others, they are convinced they can help. By absorbing the emotions and making them their own, they really believe that others will feel better if they carry their burdens for them. The problem is the adult doesn't know that the child has absorbed their emotions, and because they have not learnt to manage their feelings, they continue with patterns of limitations.

By the time we are grown adults, we are exhausted and drained by the overwhelming emotional loads we carry. To learn our lessons, we will need to give back what was not ours to take in the first place. We will discover how we are keeping unhealthy patterns in place, because others can't be responsible for themselves if we are doing all the feeling. To be fully present and responsible for ourselves, we must feel our own feelings and act from our emotional truths.

The gift of the lesson is to find the truth of our existence and come to a place of acceptance that others may have a truth different from our own. It is selfish of us to believe that everyone is the same as us, or that we are right and others are wrong about the nature of all human beings. Where we believe in oneness, the lesson will evolve us into our space of love, respect, and acceptance of all there is. Acting from the centre of love is dignity and respect, humanity and integrity towards all other people. If we treat people from our own truth, we can't be cruel or own or possess them. We can't project onto them, and we don't want to distort them because we want to meet them in that place of love, which is the place we live in.

Greed and Lack

Sometimes the lessons may validate our thinking, if we are unconscious. There will be times when it's hard to identify the real lesson, resulting in an interpretation that endorses long-held beliefs. It is possible for the injustice of selfishness to corroborate the unconscious person's sense of superiority and the need to seek to control, manipulate, and dominate others. When we lack empathy, compassion, and unconditional love, the *fear* of lack fills the gap instead. By having fear as a core emotion, there is restriction in who we are, how we express ourselves, and how we interact with others. Greed fills the void of love. Materialism fills the void of love. Brutality and violence fill the void of love. Beliefs perpetuate realities. The fear of lack sustains the desire to collect and store in excess, manifesting as greed. Lack and greed distort the ability to love, as do domination, manipulation, control, and dogmatic beliefs, attitudes, and principles.

Our response to generous, loving, and caring people reflects our connection to our own compassionate hearts.

- Some feel the need to destroy, conquer, control, or distort love
- Some have to yell and scream or be abusive and violent towards acts of love and loving people
- Some are scared by love and run away from any source of caring, gentleness, or nurturing
- Some want to have it all to themselves and so smother the giver of love
- Some want to embrace, share, and enjoy the love with gratitude

If we are of a generous nature, we may find others attracted to us in ways that could be very draining because of their fear of lack. Some people are never satisfied with what we share, and they demand more than we can give in a balanced and respectful manner. Once we understand that, we can't satisfy their need or their lack. They have this insatiable greed, and selfishly demand that their needs be met. They don't want fairness, justice, compromise, or harmony—they want it their way. No amount of giving or listening or support or compassion will ever be enough. The more we give, the more they want. We will step out of the greed game and allow for the possibility that they may face their own reality.

If the crime shows on television are to be believed, then the lesson of the injustice of selfishness has never been more valid than it is today. The shows depict people who kill a person for fear the victim will destroy or take away what they value and love, be it material possessions or people. Yet the act of killing another, result in them losing their freedom to enjoy what they hold dear. They lose it all anyway, but at their own hand and not someone else's. In this way they have created the self-fulfilling prophecy of their fear of lack: that there is not enough of what they want, and they must hold on to what they have at all cost. Their fears have not been thought through, and they haven't considered the consequences of their actions. Instead, they have been overwhelmed by their emotions and have acted irrationally. This is the internalised injustice of the outer world that feeds lack through the denial of the effective management of our emotions and feelings. If we combine our heart's desires with our logical mind and intuitive feelings to consciously act, we will choose life-affirming actions and behaviours. The positive transformation of the injustice of selfishness comes from accepting our emotions and the events in our lives by being grateful for all of it. In the end, it's up to us to hold ourselves accountable and responsible for our emotional lives.

Acceptance and Gratitude

The way through lack is acceptance and gratitude. When we can review our lives and say a thank-you to those who helped us survive the hardest bits, we find our humanity, our dignity, and our integrity. Living a consciously good life enables us to be at peace with ourselves. Being our own best friend and respecting and liking ourselves ensures we travel our journeys with confidence in our intuition, feelings, and emotions. This action enhances security in our purpose, the meaning and point of the experiences we have in our lives. By being able to replace fear with love, and to greet daily experiences ready to be aware of the opportunities as they present themselves, we will know that we still have more to learn and grow through, because life's journey is never stagnant. By embracing this reality, we will not fear those moments when we fall from our all-knowing pedestal and have to dive into our unconscious pool of surfacing memories to redo our life and its meaning all over again. We will thrive on what makes us uniquely human and utilise the emotional responses as our guiding beacons through the maze of life.

Transformation

The transformation possible from this lesson of the injustice of selfishness allows us to feel connected to our own knowing and to have strength within our emotional selves. Where we have carried another's emotions, we will learn to set boundaries and allow others to feel their own feelings. Where we have avoided acknowledging our feelings, we will instigate a journey towards emotional acceptance. We will understand our own processes and feel committed to them because they offer a sense of joy and happiness in being ourselves. We will prioritise our lives on what provides meaning and purpose. By not allowing others' demands and distractions to get in our way, the importance of setting personal boundaries will lead us to overcome our own fears of success. As we shift our perspectives, we will attract in positive experiences to develop a deeper understanding of who we truly are. We will no longer be afraid of the attention we gain for our skills, talents, or gifts, and we will feel strong within to face whatever may challenge us from within ourselves and from the outer world. We will develop our sense of knowing about universal processes, and we will connect deep in our hearts to the source of creation, believing that there is enough of everything for everyone.

CHAPTER 7

The Injustice of Vanity

'I could be anything except for the faults
I have acquired on my way.'
'Sleeping at the Wheel', Matchbox 20

THE PURPOSE OF THE INJUSTICE of vanity is to assist us in defining our sense of self and in learning how to express this identity in a balanced manner emotionally, mentally, sexually, physically, and spiritually. This journey involves Sigmund Freud's term ego as defining our soul's evolving sense of self with the Buddhist concept of the ego-mind. The lesson is about the balance between too much ego, an over-inflated sense of self with too little ego, or being self-loathing. It explores how self-sabotage is the internalisation of imperfections.

The aim of defining who we are and ensuring the self survives is constantly transforming into greater depths and complexity as we face the answers to the questions asked through this process: Who am I? Am I okay? How can I be myself and stay connected to others at the same time? How do I be true to me and still be loved and accepted by others? Why am I here? What am I meant to be doing? Within this context we will re-evaluate relationships on all levels and with all things, taking us into deeper understandings of these fundamental questions as we journey towards humility. As we embrace our humanness, we will surrender to a higher power, knowing that we can still exist within the oneness that is our true connection to all there is.

Ego as a Sense of Self

Who we are is an individual and unique manifestation of the totality of our perceived reality combined with our unconscious urges and instincts with our conscience. We spend our entire lives evolving and discovering a concept of personal identity, which is call the self. The self is what Freud referred to as the ego. The ego is the visible personality and is responsible for directing behaviour. The ego wants us to be perfect, and the need to be perfect creates the ego-mind. Having a sense of self is desirable, but once it is locked into needing to be perfect and creating rules and regulations about how this is to be achieved, we are immersed in the ego-mind.

An ego that dominates and creates imbalances occurs when we:

- Want to be good at everything
- React negatively to criticism, judgement, punishment, and condemnation
- Have expectations of everything and everyone
- Have to be in control
- Overly criticise and judge ourselves
- Say people can do as they please but then make sure our disapproval is known
- Impose our ways on others through shaming

- Happily acknowledge that there are two sides to every story—but then hold tightly to the idea that our view is the right one
- Are attached to an ideal, desire, want, or dream
- Believe that without our ego-identity, we cannot survive, think, make decisions, or function in a healthy and normal way
- Are stuck in superiority
- Believe we know what is best, right, and perfect
- Protect ourselves from facing anything that challenges our view of the world
- Are unable to accept that we have made a mistake, and so we try changing the truth into a version that makes it someone else's fault

Giving the ego-mind the power to rule our lives is an unconscious reality until we reach a point in life where we feel suffocated by its limitations and rules, choosing instead to become the master of the mind. It can take years of peeling away lies, put-downs, perceptions, and interpretations of who we thought we were and how others have treated us to enable the stepping into a balanced expression of ourselves. A sense of self that is in balance:

- Takes responsibility for words, actions, and behaviours
- Replaces fear with love, trust, faith, respect, and truth
- Accepts constructive criticism
- Self-evaluates situations and makes plans to improve and change as appropriate
- Accepts life as a process of growth
- Views everything as an opportunity to learn
- De-personalises events

he fears, insecurities, and inadequacies in others
otivate their part in interactions
...es more flexible

- Chooses to evaluate and acknowledge our own skills, talents, and gifts
- Willingly accepts its own limitations and weaknesses, knowing it is okay to be imperfect and human

The potential to feel the joy of being all we are capable of, by facing our imperfections and letting go of internal self-judgement and self-criticism, is the journey of the injustice of vanity. The elixir to ego is love—love of others and love of self. Love that is based too strongly in self or in others breeds more of the same. By introducing love into life, we discover cooperation and peace, compassion and empathy. Love that is based in a balance between self and others is the power of transformation. When we enter interactions with others from a place of love, there is no attachment to the outcomes. We are open to the potential, the possibility, and the mystery that is our daily experience. Unconditional love is a tautology. The very nature of love is that it is unconditional.

Insecurity Pattern

Through the lesson of the injustice of idleness, we explore experiences of being overlooked, being insignificant, not mattering, or being invisible as a child. The resulting pattern of viewing parents as perfect connects into the injustice of vanity when there is need to re-examine our assumptions about family dynamics to discover new insights. Perceptions and interpretations made as a child may not be completely accurate because we could not understand the motivations behind others' words or behaviours at that time.

It is innately natural for children to know they are significant, special, and magnificent. But if feeling ignored, they interpret being overlooked as being insignificant, and this distorts clear self-perception. Remembering how it felt, they have personalised feelings to mean that was the intention of the adult. This pattern then influences our adult interactions where we believe others have issues with us. An opportunity will occur to discover that everyone has insecurities, baggage from their childhood, and that things are not always as they seem. The ego-mind has to learn that sometimes everything is about us, and then at other times it has nothing to with us. How others interact with us can be influenced by a number of factors. They may:

- Envy or be jealous of us
- Love us but fear we will never love them to the same depth
- Be pre-occupied with other issues or themselves
- Feel incompetent or insecure compared to our confidence
- Be consumed with fear and worry
- Need to vent at someone and know we will forgive them
- Perceive us as strong enough to deal with their feelings
- Wish they had the courage to be authentic like we are

In fact interpretations can show three realities: first, what we think others are thinking is a reflection of how we think about ourselves; second, what others are saying is a reflection of how they feel about themselves; and third, how we think about others is a reflection of how we have been treated in the past. Each will be true in certain situations. But what is often missed in all this projecting is an acknowledgement of our value, worth, skills, talents, or gifts that are triggering fears in others. Blindness to our beauty, worth, significance, and magnificence keeps us trapped in interpreting interactions from a personal sense of lack and not being good enough. The lessons of the injustice of selfishness and vanity merge as we struggle to define who we really are, as opposed to that which we know as our soul's truth, our true self that has always existed but has been covered over by experiences in life.

The challenge is that we are convinced the people are intentionally doing this. When we feel controlled by the drama, we lose sight of the fears, insecurities, and sense of inadequacy motivating the behaviours being reacted to. These interactions hold a charge for everyone involved because people are trying to maintain their ego-minds. The desire to return to the innocence of the child that knew itself as magnificent, special, and significant feeds into these interactions. The adult seeks to be accepted, reassured, and loved and hides the vulnerability felt behind a negative exchange that is defined by a fear-filled ego-mind.

When we realise that others don't have the courage to be what they perceive we are they have no power over us. As we stand strong, projections lose the ability to negatively affect us. In this moment an amazing opportunity is provided for others to give up their false self-esteem and learn to be more honest and loving. Some will feel more exposed and up the ante in an attempt to take back the power and maintain the status quo of the relationship. But if we come from a place of strength and acknowledge it for what it is, we can choose to step out of the negativity, leaving it with them.

The Cyclic Pattern of Self-sabotage

As the brain forms, connects, and reconnects over a lifetime, we grow through phases and experience cycles of behaviours and processes. It is often easier to notice these when looking back upon reflection, but once in a state of awareness it is possible to recognise repeating patterns and change them. The lesson of the injustice of vanity connects into our patterns of self-sabotage; it cycles every nine years, influencing a two-year phase in our lives. This may be expressed as:

- Being naughty in an attempt to see if parents will still love us
- A fear of success leads to unconsciously ruining a great opportunity
- Times when traumatic shame keeps us small because we took responsibility for the actions of another
- Behaviours that are self-punishing, such as eating too much, eating things that actually make one sick, not exercising, or not taking care of an injury
- Knowing we should be doing the right thing to ourselves, and yet we don't

These everyday acts of self-sabotage result in daily lives becoming harsh and hard. We often blame external circumstances because we don't recognise the unconscious thoughts or identify the repeating patterns from earlier years. Many behaviours or patterns of self-sabotage have been formed from the interpretations of the events when we were between nine and ten years old.

The lesson of the injustice of vanity provides an opportunity to review the past and identify the beliefs formed about ourselves when nine, eighteen, twenty-seven, thirty-six, forty-five, fifty-four, sixty-three, seventy-two, and so forth. Identifying our negative self-concepts that influence our detrimental self-talk is the beginning step to break the patterns of self-sabotage. Not being able to remember blocks of time during childhood years often indicates trauma—whether it was real or perceived isn't relevant, because the brain has interpreted the experience as painful. The key is to explore the patterns present today and know that they started somewhere, often when we were nine years old.

At the age of nine, children become cognitively aware of the concept of conditional love and self-punishment. A parent's response is vital to enable them to form healthy behaviours and concepts about themselves. Recognising why children are suddenly exclaiming that a parent doesn't really love them, when the adult has never said anything like that previously, identifies the shift in brain development that allows this process. It often feels illogical to parents for their children to say this, and they dismiss it out of hand. From the children's perspective, this dismissal confirms the conditionality of love and acceptance. It is carried with them into adulthood.

Becoming conscious of the desire to self-punish through emotional eating, exercise, sexual interactions, alcohol, drugs, or severe dieting doesn't automatically break the habit. Initially this consciousness can lead to further acts of self-punishment as we shame ourselves about knowingly doing acts of self-sabotage. The lesson is to find a balanced sense of who we are through self-acceptance, self-love, and self-respect. The ability to act with compassion, kindness, and empathy assists in the finding of solutions that transform the habits and free ourselves into being our very best self possible. Learning who we are and the capacity to implement change develops inner strength and personal power. From this place of strength, ego isn't a dirty word.

Although logically it never makes sense that anyone would want to hurt themselves, the reality is that pain and human existence go hand in hand when dominated by the ego-mind. Hurting confirms we are alive. As part of the evolving self, we cycle through patterns of creating physical pain to make us feel bad about ourselves, to feel the shame locked in the unconscious. The lessons of the injustice of temptation and vanity merge because there is an escalation of experiences to make ourselves feel worse by doing something humiliating, shameful, or embarrassing. In fact what is happening is that we are personalising the external events of life and attaching the meaning, purpose, or emotion to ourselves. We are saying:

- If my parents don't want me to embarrass them, it means I'm an embarrassment
- If I am suffering through a lesson of injustice, then I must deserve to suffer
- If no one can see my hurt, then I must be worthless
- If no one will protect me, then I deserve the bad things that happen to me

The patterns of self-sabotage form when we believe circumstances are unchangeable and internalise the pain as self-punishment. By externalising the emotional pain it is felt physically, and through our behaviours, words, and actions it can be seen by others. Anything done until it hurts is a way of externalising emotional pain.

The lesson is found as we understand that behaviours are a technique of expressing the struggle experienced to give meaning of our sense of self in a balanced and moderate way.

Until we can find how we exist in harmony with those around us, we will continue to:

- Eat until it hurts
- Slash our skin to feel the pain
- Hit ourselves with things or let others hit us
- Have accidents that cause cuts or burns
- Drink until we pass out
- Take drugs in near lethal combinations
- Put ourselves in dangerous situations

Because the ego-mind wants to be the centre of attention and dominate its environment, the evolving personality must learn how to live cooperatively with the other ego-minds in families and relationships. Knowing everyone is worthwhile, lovable, valuable, and significant opens the door to unity and harmony, supporting the groundwork for the development of a balanced sense of self.

Cognitive Development Means We Need to Experience Things Twice

From the time we are conceived until twenty-five years of age, our brain is maturing into its fully developed form. This process of connecting neurons creates our personality, memories, and interpretations of the events in life. We are forming who we think we are for an entire lifetime, but the first twenty-five years sets in place the foundations from which we draw upon for meaning, purpose, and direction.

The sense of self formed before twelve and a half stems from our interactions with family, especially parents. It is about our inner world and is strongly associated with the mother principle.

On an archetypal level, the mother energy represents a place of unconditional love and acceptance, being safe and protected by a mother's love. JK Rowling captured this experience beautifully when Harry's touch had the power to dissolve evil in *The Philosopher's Stone,* because his mother's love had been so deep that it gave Harry eternal protection, an inner safety that protected him as he interacted with the outer world. This vital strength carries us into the second phase of life.

From twelve and a half to twenty-five, we become focussed in the outer world—the world of men, the patriarchy, and the father principle. On an archetypal level, the father energy represents a place of work, effort, rewards, conditions, requirements, and expectations. It is a time to put who we are out into the world and utilise gifts, talents, and skills through the efforts made in study, work, sport, and relationships. It is time to *do* something with our existence. Life is no longer simple and easy. There are no quick fixes, and a hug or a smile from a loving parent isn't enough. After having felt worthy, lovable, and special, we question these qualities and pitch them against the cultural and social norms of the world outside the family. When we are exposed to concepts of deserving, punishment, judgements, and condemnation, the harsh actuality of life enters our reality, and we have to find a place within it. By figuring out who we are within this wider world, we search for approval, acceptance, worth, and unconditional love from the external world.

Depending on whether the experiences had with peer groups, education, relationships, and work have provided positive, self-affirming concepts of self or negative, isolating, and painful interactions, we internalise all of it and create a mix of 'less than, more than' patterns about our worth and sense of self. The key here is to understand the importance of both stages in creating a full sense of who we are. We need our sense of being worthwhile, acceptable, approved of, and lovable to be met initially in the first twelve and a half years of life, and then it has to be met again in the second twelve and a half years of life for us to be whole.

Understanding the source of self-doubts, fears, insecurity, and inadequacy sheds light on how we can feel confident within yet struggle when interacting with others—or the reverse, where we achieve well in the world of work and service but feel unlovable in intimate relationships. It also explains why we can feel powerless, vulnerable, and insecure in all aspects of life. Depending on our experiences, the lesson from the injustice of vanity could permeate our entire life and be the greatest challenge, because forming a balanced sense of self is overshadowed by the need to belong.

An ego-mind can only be formed after experiencing conditional love and approval. Having been left with a gap in our sense of self fear feeds an ego-mind, filling it with self-deprecating thoughts or an inflated ego. Any events that shatter safety and connection to the family distort a sense of value in our existence. Where divorce, death, or abandonment occurs during the teenage years, the identity becomes stuck in the externalised world of others. Freud's concept of self becomes devoid of our individual ego but instead is centred entirely on what the outer world sees and interacts with. In *The Road Less Travelled* series, M. Scott Peck writes that the most resistant personality trait to heal is people who cannot accept that they are worthy just because they exist and who are permanently attached to how others treat and perceive them. Even when acknowledged as worthy, they will dismiss it as irrelevant.

An over-inflated ego can only maintain itself if others are *less than* them. But the purpose of the lesson of the injustice of vanity is to heal the wounds that created this misguided expression of self. By feeling confident, secure, and sure from within because we know we are lovable, we seek to support and maintain everyone's worth. A balanced sense of self has room for others and maintains the integrity of the core-self.

Inner Conflict

In forming ideas of who we are, there becomes an awareness of absorbed messages contributing to inner conflict. There is no requirement in the brain's memory banks that we agree with what is retained; in fact every experience is held as conscious and unconscious memory. Confusion and inner conflict is a sign that someone else's beliefs are contradicting our own thoughts and beliefs. The confusion, overwhelm, and fear stems from the inner questioning of who is right. Procrastination, defensiveness, withdrawal, isolation, and busyness become much easier than interaction with the outer world, just in case *they* are right about who we are. Being helpful, polite, passive, and subservient keeps others from getting close enough to see the real self. The aim is to avoid further judgement, opinions, and contradiction between that which our soul knows as us and the person currently presented as our identity.

The conflict exists because over time, so many layers have been built up that we don't know who we really are or how to define ourselves, except by our defence mechanisms. But we are not:

- A procrastinator
- A martyr
- Aloof
- Paranoid
- Our work

These are coping mechanisms. These are our defences to the barrage of hurt, condemnation, judgement, and conditional love endured throughout life. *But they are not who we really are.* In response to our experiences as children, we tuck our real self away. As adults, we will discover that our life purpose is to find our true self, to love and respect our real self, to accept and honour our essential self, and to value and know our core self.

Vulnerability

What if the path of humility is born from the journey of vulnerability, and when letting ourselves be 'saved' we are surrendering to a higher power—accepting our mortality, powerlessness, or limitations and allowing ourselves to be human, weak, fragile, imperfect, and unknowing? When accepting our natures in their entirety, we can learn of gratitude. Experiencing a deep, heart-felt sense of gratefulness to those who cared, saw, and loved us at our most vulnerable moments is the experience of being saved. We give thanks to those who were there by:

- Feeling empowered to continue the journey
- Graciously accepting help
- Expressing our true self and purpose
- Working towards giving back to others
- Knowing that through true service we support and maintain our humanity and global balance

By resenting weaknesses, refusing support, help, becoming angry about vulnerabilities, and denying fragility, we remain in an ego-mind prone to selfishness and being self-absorbed. When we want to be in control, always right and perfect to feel worthy, it is difficult to know of gratitude and humility. The ego-mind that is inflated, guarded, and defensive will struggle to surrender to another, let alone a higher power. The journey towards humility often comes through a crisis that shatters the illusions of grandeur.

Leaving a Legacy

At some point the realisation of our mortality impacts us. We face the possibility of death and access the desire to be remembered. The lesson asks us to consider leaving a legacy— evidence that we were here and somehow made the world a better place. By seeking to be significant and important to those we love, our families, our community, or the wider world, we remember those who have shaped our lives. As we feel the privilege of knowing these people and seek to emulate them, our life involves an aspect of service, of giving back to others.

We form a sense of community through involvement in our children's lives, sporting clubs, service clubs, volunteering, religious groups, hobbies, and interests. The value of caring for others provides us with new ways to define who we are while simultaneously enabling us to improve and enhance:

- The lives of those we love
- The experiences of the most vulnerable and disadvantaged in our society
- Environmental causes
- Animal rights

Contributing to the future caring comes in all shapes and sizes, but the act adds to the potential of a better society and a more humane approach to life.

Deserving

The lesson of the injustice of vanity is to find a balanced expression of ego, our sense of self in the world. When attached to the idea of what we deserve, it is difficult to come from a balanced sense of self. Deserving is an illusion; it makes no sense when we really think about it, but it is highly effective at keeping alive patterns of self-sabotage. Believing that what comes to us is what we deserve traps us in a reward-punishment cycle. Saying, 'You've worked hard for that promotion; you deserve it,' and 'You are a nice person and deserve to be treated well,' links effort with reward. Within itself it is a harmless association, but if deserving rewards also means deserving punishments and knowing that the ego-mind forms from experiences of conditionality, then the injustice created by a belief in *deserving* is a powerful lesson.

The saying 'I must have killed a Chinaman' implies that we have done something terrible to justify misfortune or bad luck. But when a child tells an adult about being picked on at the playground, and the first question is, 'What did you do to deserve that?' a child soon learns that it deserves the bad things that happen. Deserving is different to logical consequences and natural laws. Deserving is the belief system of the ego-mind.

The Path to Humility

In Michael Casey's *A Guide to Living in the Truth: Saint Benedict's Teaching on Humility,* he explains that over a thousand years ago, Saint Benedict proposed that humility is the truth of human nature, whereas pride is a 'radical falsehood'. This truth impacts on the mind, heart, and emotions, and to deny its influence is the source of all human suffering. Truth-filled living is the soul of humility characterised by an attitude of realism. It is a respect for the nature of things and a reluctance to force reality to conform to our emotional desires, wants, needs, and fears that lead to a life lived with humility. Saint Benedict believed we were ultimately spiritual beings and refusing to embrace this maintained suffering.

Too often it is perceived that a strong, overinflated ego is the worst character trait a person can have. Yet Saint Benedict proposed that of pride and worthlessness, it is worthlessness that is the hardest to overcome when growing towards humility. Although the process of humility is to surrender the ego and accept our incompleteness compared to God, those with a strong sense of self, attached to who they think they are, or are strongly controlled by the mind, can learn to let go over time. Those who start from a place of worthlessness misinterpret this 'incompleteness' as a personal failure, a lacking of innate value, and an absence of personal power. They are more likely to interpret their experiences as validating their insignificance and keep themselves trapped by their sense of worthlessness, thwarting them from humility instead of aligning with it.

There are two processes around the surrendering of ego. One described by Eckhart Tolle and Caroline Myss involves detaching from our ego in the form of wants, needs, desires, and dreams. They describe the event as the release of the attachment—the absoluteness of the want, need, desire, or dream. Having gone through the process, our lives are changed, and we see things differently. We are different. Our attention and focus is about not succumbing to the earthy desire again.

The second process is the one described by Saint Benedict. It is a lifelong process of peeling away layers of pride to develop our sense of humility. Here we give our attention to our daily life, living it consciously and with self-awareness. We seek to grow, learn, change, and develop our humility through the twelve steps he describes. It is a process that continues all the days of our life. Both are essential for us to develop humility. There will be times within the twelve-step process of Saint Benedict that we will need to do the surrendering of ego attachment described by Tolle and Myss; they relate to and support each other.

Putting Saint Benedict's twelve-step plan of humility into a modern context inspires us to implement the following:

The first step: Become conscious of our words, deeds, thought, and actions.

- Become aware of why we act the way we act
- Become aware of why we think what we think
- Become aware of why we feel how we feel
- Become aware of why we do what we do
- Explore our fears, doubts, and insecurities, as well as our love, passion, desire, and will for what we want

The second step: Become responsible for all of who we are.

- Accept who we are and its impact on our own life and others
- Learn that our will and desire does not dictate life here for us or others
- Begin to share equally in joy, pleasure, hardships, and pain
- Acknowledge our role in everything and acknowledge others role in everything as well
- Step out of the drama and acknowledge how we control ourselves and others through drama

The third step: Acknowledge a higher power.

- Learn that we are not God; we don't decide what is best for others and deem it so
- Accept that we can't control every event in our life
- Learn to pray, talk to, and seek guidance from God, Spirit, a higher power, or all there is
- Surrender our will to divine will

The fourth step: Patience in enduring difficulties with equanimity.

- Learn to be patient
- Accept that we do not determine the timing of events
- Learn the lesson that all things are as they should be in any given moment
- Learn to endure hard times and still be happy

The fifth step: Self-revelation.

- Face our own imperfections and admit them to those we have hurt because of them
- Do not seek forgiveness for our imperfections; merely accept our responsibility
- Accept how others feel about our words, actions, and beliefs, and feel how human we really are

The sixth step: Contentment with the least of everything.

- Learn to be grateful for all we have, and let go of the desire for the best and biggest of everything
- Find joy in the little things in life

- Learn to value family and friends for who they are, without wanting them to change in ways we desire

The seventh step: Awareness of our own liabilities.

- See ourselves as the smallest and most insignificant human being on the planet, and enjoy it for what it is
- Embrace our powerlessness and free ourselves from the fear we will not survive
- Stop taking everything personally
- Accept that everything isn't about us
- Accept that 'deserving' is ego, and there is no such thing as deserving what we get—good, bad, or indifferent

The eighth step: Seek to understand oneness.

- Learn that we are not alone, that we are not an island
- Learn that we are not one individual striving to succeed and conquer all others
- Learn about love. There is no such thing as unconditional love because love is unconditional—anything less, and it is conditional love
- Develop empathy and compassion for the human reality
- Embrace the concepts of unity, oneness, connection, and harmony as the way of living in our daily life

The ninth step: Learn silence and stillness.

- Learn not to advise others on their life
- Learn to hold our tongue and listen with compassion
- Even if we know a lot about a topic, practice not sharing this information as an expert

- Stop idle chatter
- Learn to be peaceful in thought, feeling, and actions
- Develop a balance in our use of energy

The tenth step: Avoidance of laughter.

- Stop dismissing things that matter to us and others
- Stop making jokes at others expense or our own
- Stop minimising ours and others hurts and pains

The eleventh step: Gravity in speech

- Use fewer words when we speak
- Only say what must be said
- Speak softly, clearly, and concisely
- Step out of the mindless storytelling and do not repeat rumours and untruths
- Never gossip

The twelfth step: Humility.

- Be humility in body and heart—in all that is said or done
- Surrender the need to be seen to be humble
- Accept that we don't define ourselves as humble, but others see us as humble in our words and actions

Having reached the final step, we are now free to ascend to the perfect love of God, which casts out all fear. Through this love, all that we once observed with fear, we will now fulfil without effort, as though naturally from habit. Fear will be replaced by love.

By shedding emotional baggage, releasing the hold fear has, and stepping into the creative void of possibility, we will give birth to ourselves. We will shift our language from choosing, seeking, and desiring to *becoming* all that we are— an ever-changing, ever-evolving person enjoying a sense of completeness—before discovering the next layer. We will feel like our existence has become gentler, subtler, and more fine-tuned with an awareness of how we use our energy. In our stages of self-containment, we will accept the need for isolation as we solidify who we are. We will feel strong in our new awareness of self and will venture back into the world to learn how to maintain who we are in the busyness of life and the demands of work, relationships, children, and friendships.

Transformation

The transformation possible from the lesson of the injustice of vanity is to embrace our whole self, accepting imperfections and knowing our worth simply because we exist. Enjoying a sense of ease and wholeness from feeling more confident, self-reliant, and self-assured enables us to calmly but firmly set boundaries. We will know who we are as a separate entity; if blending with others is a statement of who we are, then we exist within the oneness. We will travel our journey towards humility, releasing the control of our ego-mind each step of the way. We will arrive at a level of self-acceptance that will transform our pain, life, and existence. Through self-acceptance we will naturally extend this to acceptance to others. It is when we respect our freedom to think, feel, and act in ways that express our truth that we will respect others' rights to do the same, providing it doesn't violate another's right to live and be safe.

Facing the meaninglessness and pointlessness of life will enable us to let go of our unwanted baggage as we become free to define ourselves and decide on our future. Illnesses, behaviours, or afflictions that have been created to avoid fully expressing who we are will be transformed. We will connect into our power of choice and feel liberated in our newly found freedom. Our desire to participate fully in life and accept our incarnation into our physical body will assist us in recognising how we have been living a spiritual life without the spirituality. We will move deeper into our connection with God as we work through the truth of who we are.

CHAPTER 8

The Injustice of Intimidation

'Don't you know this is just a competition; the
winner is the one who hits the hardest.'
'Please Don't Leave Me', Pink

THE PURPOSE OF THE LESSON of the injustice of intimidation
is to assist us to explore the degrees of violation that exist in
society. Living in denial about the impact we have on others
and struggling to understand why violation of space, worth,
integrity and dignity occur in response to selfish, insecure,
jealous, angry, hostile, defensive, silent, or aloof behaviours
consumes daily conversations. As we identify just how hurtful
violating actions, words, and deeds are, we become aware of
the wounds, wrong-doings and blame we are carrying from
our past.

It is easy to identify how others have impacted us—the
challenge is accepting the impact we have on others. The
saying 'How people feel about what you say is their problem'
supports us in removing our societal and social responsibility for
behaviours and words. But it is in our response to knowing how
others feel about our actions, behaviours, and words that bring

forth the lesson of intimidation. Our *versions of violence* will need to be explored while working through our relationship to anger, rage, frustration, impatience, hostility, defensiveness, withdrawing, or using silence to control and manipulate others. At the same time, we will explore how these tactics are used by others and impact on us.

Versions of Violence

In her song 'Versions of Violence', Alanis Morissette provides a list of violent acts towards another. Many of our daily interactions with others reflect her message that the absence of healthy, productive communication based in love rather than fear creates our hurts in relationships. This song is all about the injustice of intimidation; as her chorus says, 'These versions of violence, sometimes subtle, sometimes clear, and the ones that go unnoticed still leave their mark once disappeared.' Realistically, experiencing attacks or violations to the core of who we are leaves a mark. Years after the experience, the memory is trapped as a trauma in the unconscious mind, continuing to feed back the hurt and the perception formed about us at that time.

The one causing the pain for another often tries to dismiss the impact as:

- Everyone does this; it's normal
- It didn't really hurt them
- I was justified; they deserved it
- They were asking for it

When we internalise the violation and blame ourselves for it, we begin to violate our own souls.

Anger

Anger is the fight component of the adrenal glands physiological fight-flight response; its purpose is to motivate self-protective action. In reality, anger can be expressed in a variety of ways. We may:

- Internalise anger and self-sabotage
- Vent anger out toward others and society as violence, rage, and destruction
- Deny our anger, suppressing it into the unconscious and creating illness instead
- Use the awareness of the anger as a message that something isn't okay in our life

In *The Dance of Anger,* Harriet Goldhor-Lerner explains that if we can accept that anger indicates something is wrong—about not having our needs met, or giving up too much of ourselves for others, or doing too much for others at our and their expense—then we can make choices. We can identify the real issues and the triggers to anger. This allows responses to experiences instead of reactions.

Responses that are creative, flexible, and positive support an open mind, ensuring finding a solution that is adaptable and innovative. Humour is a vital aspect to good decision making and solution finding, yet anger and humour tend to exclude each other. Anger burns up energy, making people tired. Humour fires up our energy, making us feel light, happy, and enthusiastic.

Anger is a misunderstood emotion; we are wired to feel anger just as we are wired to feel fear. Its call to action can change current situations. By listening to and observing anger, we can utilise the energy in a positive and creative manner. It is only as we learn to manage emotions and work with them, rather than against them or let them run all responses, that we will feel empowered by self-awareness. Observing feelings, exploring the triggers, understanding the unconscious collective experiences, and making choices about how we will respond to any given situation transforms our lives and sense of self-mastery.

There are two kinds of anger: identity anger and anger as a secondary emotion. Discovering the anger felt when who we are is violated is different from feeling angry as an expression of another emotion. An example is when we feel hurt and express it as anger rather than hurt. This is what is meant as anger as a secondary emotion: it is the emotion conveyed on behalf of the real emotion.

Identity Anger

We are all born as valuable, worthy, important, significant, and magnificent beings, yet the experiences we have may not reinforce this to us. When we are treated in unfair and unjust ways that erode a sense of self, we will experience identity anger, which is when our self-concept has been violated and the anger stimulates actions that reflect an inner-knowing that we exist and we matter. Through the generations, childhood experiences often left children feeling like they did not matter and were non-existent. The mottos 'Children should be seen but not heard', 'Children bounce back', and 'They get over it' are just some examples of child-raising attitudes that many have experienced. Anger proves these are myths and untrue. In fact as children, the way in which they coped was by feeling angry and withdrawing some part of their innocence, vulnerability, trust, and gentleness from how they interacted with the world. They toughen up and therefore lost the joy in life.

Identity anger is felt when:

- Our power, control, and choice are taken away from us
- We are not recognised for our skills and abilities
- We are only there to please others with a lack of awareness of our needs
- Judgements and limitations are placed on how okay we are

This is core, primary anger and is essential to motivate self-protective action. By channelling the energy of anger into positive, life-affirming action, it can become an enhancing emotion. In time anger will give way to passion and determination as our sense of self feels more secure. If we stop being angry about being violated, we will become broken and switch off the innate, self-protective mechanisms in the body. To understand responses to identity anger, we need to explore what happened when, as children, we felt our core self was being violated and we expressed self-protective anger. Three key responses from authority figures would have been to punish, support, or praise and encourage the reactions.

Punished

If we were punished for standing up for ourselves, we may interpret that others think we are unimportant and therefore worthless. This would feed into a sense of powerlessness. The anger may end up being internalised, suppressed, and concentrated in the body as bitterness and resentment. Imposing self-limiting conditions when around others would mean conversations would be stifled and behaviours would be restricted. We may only do things that please others. We keep our real nature to ourselves. Alternatively, we may choose to rebel, becoming uncooperative and hostile to anyone we perceive as threatening our sense of self.

Praised and Encouraged

If we were praised and encouraged in child-like expression of anger, we may have become bullies, dominating and intimidating others to get our own way and to assert our rights and needs. We may throw temper tantrums even as adults, or we use violence (emotional, verbal, or physical) as a way to express ourselves, declaring that we have an uncontrollable temper. Rage, violence, manipulation, control, and power imbalances are not only destructive on those who it is inflicted upon, but they destroy the person who does it; this is how we create our own injustice.

Supported

Where we were supported, we would feel respected and powerful; by having our sense of self reinforced, we'd feel worthy and valuable. We knew that a sense of fairness and justice existed in the world, and we would feel safe and strong when facing other issues in our lives that confront our safety and security.

As adults we can find the balance between the reality of life—its ugliness and harshness—with the joy, excitement, and passion of our true natures. The lesson of the injustice of intimidation provides an opportunity to re-evaluate all the past wrongs we experienced. By processing hurt rather than letting it build up, we can forgive, let go, and move on. It is important to learn our lessons and not constantly repeat mistakes. This maintains freshness in greeting new experiences but allows for aware and wise interactions.

Assertiveness occurs when we stand in our own needs and rights, and at the same time we respect others' rights and needs as equal to our own. No one's needs are more important, and no one has rights at the expense of another. This means that power is shared, control is balanced, and no one is violated.

Violation, Apologies, and Excuses

One of the most confronting lessons of the injustice of violation is when we have been physically bashed, sexually raped, and mentally and emotionally abused. Each of these is a violation of our core identity, integrity, and dignity. We have every right to be angry at the injustice and choices someone else has made. Often society tries to make excuses for the perpetrator of the violation; even the court system takes into consideration the background of offenders when sentencing them. The perpetrators chose to act in a certain way—there can be no justification. Consequences are needed so that those violated feel protected by societal values.

There are some who believe that if a perpetrator says sorry, or if the violated person can be made to understand why the perpetrator acted that way, it will somehow magically help the healing of abuse and violation. In fact, this adds to the injustice and a sense of violation. Not only have we been violated by the perpetrator, but now we are being violated by the system, society, friends, and family, depending on who is involved with the minimisation, justification, or dismissal of our experience. Today people are so focused on finding an explanation for *why* people act the way they do that they forget to validate our pain.

By accepting the apology or the context of the abuse, the person internalises a sense of blame and responsibility for what happened. By running a story that says, 'It's okay what happened to us,' or, 'It doesn't matter anymore'—or worse, becoming friends with the people who have violated them because of the pressure of family, friends, or schools—the injustice is maintained. The person is violating his own integrity and dignity. They are being forced to act with disrespect towards their core self. It is essential that the responsibility of the violation remain with the person who did it.

Even if we receive an apology or an explanation of what caused the violating event, we are allowed to feel our feelings about that situation. Accepting context or an apology does not take away the reality that it happened and that it mattered to us. It does matter, because *we* matter. By suppressing the experience, we push the memory and the trauma into the unconscious mind, where it sits vibrating away and attracting in more of the same kind of experiences; we have given up on our worth, respect, dignity, and integrity. We have to be allowed to choose to forgive our perpetrators when it feels right for us to do so.

Learning the lessons of the injustice of intimidation will lead to the healing of old wounds and the reprocessing of stored trauma, transforming and reimprinting new and more positive approaches to life. It often comes through a crisis of physical, emotional, or mental health. Rarely do our violations remain suppressed for an entire lifetime. The patterns created to survive and preserve what is left of our core self are usually dysfunctional.

By internalising the original violation, the self-blame leads to an acceptance and tolerance of a level of pressure, stress, strain, violation, and abuse as normal. Unconsciously, what we have created is a belief that we are strong enough to cope with any amount of wrongdoing; therefore our personal boundaries will be porous, and we will allow in more toxic experiences than is healthy. If we surrender to the intimidation, violation, or abuse as a way to release the pressure, we give in and let the person have what they want. Surrendering has become a way to survive because we convince ourselves that it is better than breaking. While watching those who don't surrender but continue to fight, we notice how they fight until they break— or if they don't break, they become the violator because they don't know how to stop fighting.

A Competitive Society

The challenge with this lesson is that Western capitalist society has a basic philosophy of winners and losers. It is a competitive way of thinking, and by its very nature it is unfair and unjust. The focus is on winning, not on value or skills or abilities. When we become dogmatically positioned and justify rigidity with the argument that we were right because we won, we create and maintain injustice.

A competitive society means that as individuals, we don't want fairness for all, justice for all, compromise, or harmony, instead, we want it totally and solely our way. We become submerged in *a dog eat dog world*. When anyone dares to threaten this reality, people explode physically, verbally, emotionally, and sexually, or they do silent treatments to punish others. This is the link between the injustice of selfishness and intimidation. A fear of lack feeds anger, rage, defensiveness, and the desire to be violent and intimidate those feared most. Stepping out of the rat race takes courage. Being willing to find our personal truth and live our lives accordingly is the first step in transforming this lesson.

Lessening the Anger

By remembering that life is a stage and we are all actors, we can explore what triggers those phases of seriousness. The more 'shoulds' and 'should nots', 'oughts' and 'ought nots', and 'meant to bes' we have, the more serious life becomes. The more structure and rules applied, the more serious life becomes. The more attached we are to the outcomes in life, the more serious life becomes. The less flexible we are, the less likely we are to adapt to life in productive ways that will create what we desire. Relaxing, enjoying experiences, and being grateful naturally lead to less anger. A philosophy that frees us from expectations of perfection and labelling everything as either right or wrong would let us approach life like a two-year-old: curious about everything, excited about new experiences, and staying connected with our most innocent, vulnerable, and gentle self. Life remains fresh and new. Anger, bitterness, and resentment dominate our personalities because it hurts to be kind, innocent, trusting, and vulnerable to others.

Daunted by Others

When we feel intimidated by those who have great beauty, skill, knowledge, wealth, and charisma, our lack of worth triggers a need to compare ourselves to them. We find ourselves *wanting* as we view ourselves as ugly, plain or having a beige personality, lacking in skills and knowledge that are of any value to the society, and never earning enough money. This sense of ordinariness is accompanied with fears, self-doubt, insecurity, jealousy, or envy of the person admired.

The lesson of the injustice of intimidation is found in the response to our self-criticism. Many will want to diminish this person's natural gifts by acting against them. In Jewel's song *Pieces of You*, she refers to this aspect within us, where we think nasty thoughts, say hurtful things, call people names, damage people's reputations, stereotype them, blame them for being born, hate them, and at the most extreme violate them, physically harm them, or kill them. We do this so that we can feel safe. It is the ego-mind that fears the consequences of not being the perfect, desired one. Yet with such violence projected towards these people, who would ever choose to be beautiful, successful, or charismatic?

Many will desire to be like those we admire by *attaching* to them in the hope that some of their knowledge, appeal, skills, and shine will rub off. We are drawn to the beautiful, articulate, intelligent people of the world and act as if we, too, are like them. But we are not them. Eventually we will need to acknowledge who we are and our own gifts to share with the world. Celebrating others' gifts frees the space for self-acceptance. While we deny who we are, we are denying who others are; self-injustice creates injustice for others. By accepting that differences are okay and that there are no perfections in the human race, just a collection of qualities that create certain outcomes at certain times and in certain ways, we can appreciate all of humanity's gifts.

Competition and Competitors

To explore the patterns of the injustice of intimidation, it becomes important to identify the emotional triggers to the reaction. Common emotions like jealousy, envy, fear, insecurity, and self-doubt create intimidating responses. Not valuing, believing, or acknowledging our skills, talents, and abilities means we not only look at others with envy and jealousy, but we judge and condemn them to distance ourselves from those insecurities. The act of condemnation and judgement is an act of intimidation; it is also how we are creating an injustice for other people. They aren't doing anything other than being their authentic self. They may not even see themselves the way we do, and so the negativity towards them will be baffling, confusing, and bewildering. Once they internalise this injustice, they think that they:

- Have done something wrong
- Are not okay expressing their personality
- Are bad for whatever we have judged them for
- Don't have a skill, gift, or talent that is worthwhile

They will then change how they behave, and this links into the injustice of limitations because our intimidation restricts their ability to be all they can be.

By not seeing our own worth, we are creating an injustice for ourselves despite the fact that we may blame others for how we feel. An example of this is how women have their sexuality or sex appeal labelled as whores, sluts, or prostitutes. Too many times these labels come from other women because they view each other as competitors for men's attention. Often women believe they can't attract a man by being themselves. They do not see their beauty, how feminine and desirable the female body is, the joy of an intelligent conversation, and how enticing a self-confident woman is to men. They resort to competing for men's attention, trying to draw men in by putting themselves on display by dressing in tight, skimpy, low-cut clothes and leaving nothing to the imagination. They pretend to be worthy and confident behind the façade of desirability.

When faced with other women who don't do this, and by observing how men are drawn to them, jealousy, envy, insecurity, and anger surface. They become infuriated that the effort put in is not gaining the results intended, and these other women have men swooning and falling other themselves for their attention, so the women call the others sluts, spread rumours about their sexual activity, accuse them of sleeping with every man in town, and call them names to their face.

But everything thought and said about another woman is only a reflection of the one saying it. Creating an injustice for them ultimately creates an injustice for us. It also creates an injustice for men, because women limit them with labels of only being interested in women for sex. Human interactions are far more complicated than this, and denying the reality of individual appeal, attraction, and intrigue feeds the lessons of the injustice of intimidation for all involved.

Then there is what men do to women from their source of insecurity, jealousy, envy, and anger. When a man is attracted to a woman, and she has the attention of other men, his jealousy spurs not just unfair and unjust behaviours, words, and deeds towards the woman, but also the other men in an attempt to intimidate them to stay away from her. Many men believe that they can win the heart of a woman through intimidation and by playing mind games, putting them down, trying to make them feel insecure, and inducing self-doubt by commenting on everything from the hair on their body to their beliefs, occupation, friends, and how they choose to live lives.

When women don't feel worthy at their core, these interactions damage them. They create insecurities, and this is exactly what the men are trying to do. Because the man feels insecure, by creating the same feeling in the woman, he is attempting to gain power and self-confidence through making the woman feel worse. By comparison, the man feels more worthy than the woman in his mind. She will limit her self-expression, and the man has won and maintains his view that he is better than the woman. This is how power games develop and maintain themselves in relationships: they stem from insecurity. Fear, doubts, jealousy, envy, and insecurity are the fodder that feeds the injustice of intimidation.

The adage that love is blind is true, but so is rage. In seeking a mate, women tend to idolise men. Science has not yet concluded whether this is the effects of the biological imperative to reproduce the species with the best genetic material possible or just human nature, but the lesson of the injustice of intimidation is found in the response women have when their rose-coloured glasses are removed, and they see the man as he is and may well have always been. The woman's scorn, wrath, and vindictiveness towards her mate are seen in her need to make him suffer. This creates his injustice. The man best suited to procreate children with doesn't always turn out to be the best man with whom to raise the children. By taking responsibility for choices and accepting biological, social, and personal needs, and how these influence decisions, men and women have an opportunity to transform their illusions of each other.

The entire purpose of life's lessons is to comprehend our choices and responsibility while at the same time acknowledging others' choices and responsibilities. Emotionally processing the impact of choice enables us to learn lessons. It is important to feel what is felt, own it, and be responsible for the consequences of the choices made when expressing our understanding of life. When we learn from experiences by moving on with an open heart—transforming anger, hurt, and shame into compassion

and respect for self and others—it becomes
beyond the role injustice plays in life an
transpersonal meaning behind events.

Relationships and the Lesson of Intimᵤᵤ.

All human interactions provide the ingredients to experience the full gamut of life's lessons. Being exposed to injustices provides opportunities to grow into our best possible self . . . or to plunder into the abyss of self-destruction and negativity. The adventure of connecting and relating to others is the place of life education. Running away from one bad experience in an attempt to avoid the pain usually only finds us in another interaction with the same themes. Relationships that are intimidating and violating of our sense of self are often those that manifest themselves over and over in our lives. Learning to set healthy boundaries and develop a positive and strong sense of self that is respectful may take a lifetime to cultivate.

How we are treated by others does not always reflect our conscious beliefs; it stems from a number of contributing factors. First, who we think we are; second, what actions are acceptable to us; and third, how others treat us. These beliefs form from how we were treated as a child. Early socialisation was done *to us* and was not of our choosing. Due to how brains function up to the age of thirteen, we have little control over the adults who influence these formative years. The child's world is one of fantasy, illusion, creativity, and imagination because children function from the right side of the brain. That is why children believe in Santa Claus and the Easter Bunny. It is why they believe their parents are perfect. It is also why they believe in goodness and think that they are the centre of the world.

Wanting to punish ourselves for how we thought and acted as a child becomes pointless if we are seeking to make sense of our lives. The more we beat ourselves up for being a child, the more we are creating the injustice of intimidation to ourselves, and therefore we are maintaining its presence in our outer world. We need to look back at our childhoods with love, compassion, and understanding for the child's reality.

How we are treated during these formative years becomes the unconscious data that filters all experiences after turning thirteen. What happens during our teenage years solidifies, dissolves, or creates whole new interpretations of who we are and how we should be treated. By bringing the full gamut of experiences with us into adulthood, we have a varied and complex array of memories that contribute to how we are treated by others, how we treat ourselves, and how we treat the people in our lives. When we explore our relationships, what we find is:

- That people treat us how we let them treat us
- That people treat us how we treat ourselves
- That people treat us based on who they are

The resistance is often expressed to the idea that people *treat us based on who they are.* But how often have we received a present from someone and realised that it is *their* taste and not ours? They haven't thought about who we are and what we like; they have bought the present they would like to receive. This simple act imparts a sense of invisibility, of being unseen and even overlooked. It hurts, and when the hurt builds up, we usually turn it into anger to find a way to voice our disappointment, our desire to be noticed and acknowledged, that we really do matter and exist.

Healthy Sharing of Self

When forming relationships with other
ourselves, and this is normal. But where

- People give so much of themselves to one person that
  they don't have anything left for others,
- A person shares little or nothing of themselves with
  others, or
- One person controls another's life totally, then an
  unhealthy relationship is in existence.

Society doesn't display healthy relationships as the norm.
Television and movies are filled with romantic versions of
marriage and families were they merge with each other. Sitcoms
show people putting each other down constantly and it having
no negative impact on them. This is not what *real* people
experience in real life. The reality is we want to be loved and
accepted by others, and we get hurt when we are not. Personal
boundaries must be respected for us to feel whole, worthwhile,
and valued by others.

Although we must learn to respect ourselves, the capacity
to do this reflects past experiences. The ability to truly value
ourselves as worthy and whole comes after the brain has fully
developed at the age of twenty-five.

Abuse does not exist where respect of physical, emotional,
mental, sexual, and spiritual boundaries occurs. There is no
mistaking an abusive relationship compared to a non-abusive
relationship. The problem is that so many relationships are
abusive—if not physically or sexually, then emotionally,
mentally, or spiritually. It is a violation because that's what
intimidation does: it violates our soul.

After having been in relationships that violate our sense self, it is harder to share parts of our inner self with others in a balanced, respectful, and moderate manner. Poor, inconsistent, or a complete lack of internal boundaries present as:

- Sharing too much of ourselves with others, thus continuing to experience further violations
- Violating others' space by trying to take up too much of their energy
- Trying to fix things for them when they haven't given us permission to do so
- Only being able to feel safe by excluding people completely, because we need all our energy or resources for ourselves
- Wanting to control everything about someone else

Sharing becomes challenging. Instead, we:

- Give ourselves over in our entirety
- Bounce back and forth in giving and blocking people out of our lives
- Block people out completely, forming very few meaningful connections

It is the inconsistency that leaves interactions feeling complicated and confusing. The aim for everyone is to maintain a sense of safety and security. The reality is frustration when dealing with this chaos and a sense of abandonment, rejection, and disrespect.

Predators

Predators are people who seek power and control another for the sole purpose of having their physical, sexu emotional, or mental needs met. A key element to predato thinking is the need to dominate the people they can and to ignore those they can't. They have the capacity to use human nature—the need to be loved, liked, and accepted—as a weapon against their prey. Concepts of love are distorted because they believe that the only way they can be loved is by controlling others and placing conditions on them. They hope conditionality makes others want them more, and the very act of controlling another induces subservience, duty, and obligation rather than love, respect, and honour.

Predators have no power over those who don't need them to feel worthwhile, valued, acceptable, or loved. This is often confusing and bewildering to the predators, because a core belief they have is that everyone needs others to love them in order to enable them to feel lovable. It is a foreign concept that someone could feel lovable, acceptable, worthy, and valuable from within.

Being raised in the presence of predators creates a survival mentality and patterns of creating a sense of safety. This includes behaviours such as

- Energetically attaching to the predator to ensure an awareness of others' motivations and behaviours
- Demanding others meet needs through being needy and clingy
- Being a bully and intimidating others into submission
- Playing the victim

Learning about human nature teaches us about our own natures.

Just Have to Do or Say Things

'man nature that means people have
are best not articulated. No matter
stop them, they will still do it. There are
not said because of the consequences they will
are relationships that are sacred, and violating that
creates great pain for all involved

- The bond of monogamy in marriage
- The balance of power between authority figures and those they have authority over, such as a teacher and a student, a policeman and a victim of crime, a minister of religion and the congregation
- The unconditional love between a parent and the child

Sacred relationships should always be upheld.

The lesson of the injustice of intimidation brings an awareness and understanding that the person with the desire is convinced that the other feels the same way. This is why people feel the need to say how they feel and what they desire out loud, or to take action on their desires. Learning about how people objectify and sexualise as a reflection of their fears, insecurities, shame, self-doubt, and inadequacies is confronting and disturbing, but the anger felt about such desires and the unnecessary need to express those desires only intertwines those objectifying with those objectified.

The more one blames and shames the other, the more rigid the attachment becomes to each other. When we take full responsibility for ourselves and realising that everything comes down to the choices made, we can transform the bonds of

subjection. By coming to the realisation that ;
are there for us to learn about ourselves rathei
to action, we gain a sense of self-control. Act
others who we are as we disentangle from b
longer reflect the choices they make about us

Ignoring and the Core Self

In his rice experiment, Masaru Emoto proves the violence
inherit in ignoring that someone exists. He conducted an
experiment with school children and rice. He had three rice
grains and had the children interact with them differently:

- One rice grain was told that it loved and how wonderful
  it was
- One rice grain was told it was hated
- One rice grain was completely ignored

The impact on each rice grain was that the one receiving
the children's loving words grew and was healthy. The rice
grain told that it was hated grew but then turned mouldy
and black, and it died. The rice grain that was completely
ignored and therefore received no attention never grew and
simply died. Emoto concluded that being ignored is the most
aggressive act a person can do to another. Withholding energy,
attention, and love from another is the most devastating form
of violence to a person. As human beings, we need a sense
of connection, belonging, and interaction with each other; it
isn't natural to live isolated lives. The desire to do this and our
ability to succeed in it reflects the damage done through all of
the injustices, not just intimidation.

lating to the Core Self

Exploring when human interactions are enmeshed with fear and anger will help face those times that have been devastating to our core self. As illusions about those we loved, cared about, or wanted acceptance from are shattered, we will open up to the layers of suppressed memories and re-evaluate our lives. Upon realising that those we thought would honour us have ended up violating us, we will access the depth of pain, hurt, and betrayal. Confronting the deepest questioning of who we are, and even how we are seen, challenges the foundations of our perceived reality.

When we realise that these experiences destroyed our confidence and belief in ourselves, as well as our knowledge and trust in the world around us, we will find that everything that was once secure becomes insecure. Everything known becomes unknown. We will be forced to face how abandoned, ignored, and overlooked we felt. At the very moment something should have been about us, they violated our vulnerability and dismissed us as irrelevant. We will feel as if we were there to be their punching bag and to be concerned about them and their pain. It will be a feeling of a lifetime consuming us—a lifetime of betrayal, of every major event in our childhood, of all those times that our core self had felt violated over and over again. As we feel our way through the pain, we will heal our deepest wounds and discover the power of forgiveness and self-acceptance.

Taking Off the Blinders

Evolving through this lesson we will begin to move from the adrenals fight-flight response and into heart-centred energy to express love, compassion, and empathy for ourselves and others. By freeing interactions of judgement, condemnation, and punishment, we become conscious of the interplay of patterns, needs, and desires active in our lives. Identifying what is not expressed outright by others enables the awareness of the seething anger, frustration, and irritability underlining many relationships. Forming bonds that are claimed to be mutual but are really a front from the other person to focus on them will no longer trap us in a sense of loyalty, duty, or obligation.

We may even choose to step out of the role of protecting someone from themselves, because we recognise that we are a source of irritation. Expending great energy to hide someone's bad behaviours feeds our irritation, and while at the same time the person feels annoyed because they don't understand why we are doing this. We are not serving others by preventing them from having to face the consequences of their own personality, words, or deeds. As we find the courage to name the cause of the smouldering anger out loud (with love and compassion), we will give others back the responsibility of their own lives—and with it, we embrace our personal responsibilities.

Transformation

The transformation possible from the lesson of the injustice of intimidation will allow who we really are to be expressed. We will feel natural and comfortable within ourselves. Our persona may be perceived as expanded, and our confidence will be noticeable. When we are self-assured and self-confident, we know who we are, are able to discern experiences, and aren't interested in justifying any of this to others. We feel no need to explain ourselves, and others' perception will not limit us in the same ways. When we are able to easily recognise our anger when judged or limited, we will have the inner strength to stand firmly in our right to be who we are without violating another's rights or needs.

We may not tolerate people treating us poorly, and we will act to assert how we *do* wish to be treated. We will no longer accept apologies by minimising experiences. Although we will learn to forgive ourselves and others with compassion, we will not forget the lessons learnt. We will leave the responsibility for wrongdoing where it belongs, and we will develop an understanding of people's lives without falling into being a victim to social and cultural conditioning. By connecting into natural rhythms, balancing energy flow, and using our love and passion to motivate instead of hinder, we will transcend the struggle in daily life.

CHAPTER 9

The Injustice of Emotionality

*'You owe me nothing for giving the love that
I give; you owe me nothing for caring the way
that I have; I bet you're wondering when my
conditional police will force you to cough up.'*
'You Owe Me Nothing in Return', Alanis Morissette

THE PURPOSE OF THE INJUSTICE of emotionality is to assist us with issues of truth and authenticity in who we are. Too often as a society we simplify people down to stereotypes, categories, and labels. The expectations of our roles as mother, father, daughter, son, teacher, nurse, doctor, lawyer, construction worker, receptionist, draftsman, volunteer, artist, and so forth define who we are—yet none of these definitions or expectations adequately explains an individual. The complexity of love, relationships, interactions, intentions, needs, and motivations further overlay the reality of who anyone is. Deeply submerged in who we are lies our concepts of giving to others and our capacity to receive love, nurturing, and support. The collective experiences of childhood influences our interpretations, our assumptions, and our potential, adding further complexity and depth to how we access the truth of who we are and our capacity to be authentic with others.

Love, Needs, and Niceness

Rarely will someone openly say, 'I'm not a nice person. I'm selfish. I'm deceptive. I love to lie and manipulate people. Nothing makes me happier than intimidating someone, and I'm proud of how I live my life by being like this.' Most people think they are nice. They think they act in ways that are kind, caring, and giving to others. Intention and self-perception colour the formation of a sense of self, of the purpose behind any actions taken or words spoken. In the search for inner truth and authenticity, conscious thoughts and intentions are not sufficient to justify motivations and actions. The unconscious mind feeds thinking processes in ways that are initially undetected. Because we believe the story that is consciously running, we don't question the source of the beliefs or experiences that have contributed to how we interpret our lives; this creates a conflict between what we believe we are saying and doing, and how others experience our words and actions.

The Need to Be Loved as a Motivator

Love is at the core of all experiences. It is the greatest need, and when met, it leads to a feeling that all other needs are met. At the same time, if any need is not met, we will feel unloved in addition to the unmet need. Those emotional needs include the following.

| Acceptance | Approval | Worthiness | Respect |
| Being wanted | Belonging | Safety | Visibility |

Encouraged	Significant	Trust	Supported
Security	Competence	Purpose	Connection
Independence	Sensuality	Wholeness	Freedom

If love entwines all these needs together unconsciously, our minds will link dozens of experiences to intensify our feelings of being loved or not loved. When we seek to feel loved and have needs met through interactions with friends, family, partners, bosses, colleagues, and the community, we will unconsciously place conditions on these interactions. Until we love ourselves, we will contaminate all actions with the need to be loved by others.

The Receiver's Experience

As the receiver of conditional giving, the tainted gift is unwanted because there is an awareness of what is expected.

- Give something back to the person
- Behave in a certain way to make the person happy
- Say certain words in response to the kindness

Receivers would rather not be 'helped' due to the array of emotional responses attached to the conditions of the kindness, caring, giving, or love. They commonly feel angry, guilty, suffocated, imposed upon, inconvenienced, resentful, frustrated, annoyed, irritated, and guilted into thanking or conforming to the giver—and all along they never wanted what was given or how it was given.

Depending on the pressure and the type of relationship, receivers are made to feel bad for having their own needs and wanting them met in a way that suits them. In response they:

- Toughen up
- Put a layer of guarded distance between themselves and the giver
- Become aloof
- Feel angry, resentful, and bitter at how others can't respect their boundaries and needs
- Feel that their dignity has been disrespected
- Withdraw from others
- Use isolation as a safe place to be, because then no one else can impose on them or take away their dignity

The Giver's Response

The lesson of the injustice of emotionality is prevalent where the realisation that:

- Giving to others is motivated by a need to be loved
- A feeling of not being worthy is being denied through doing things for others
- Acts of service come from a need to be accepted and approved of

This will be confirmed when givers are angry with the other person for not giving back the love, appreciation, gratitude, material rewards, or the same kind of devotion they believe they have given. Ultimately, giving with the expectation that love needs will be met is conditional giving. The lesson will be intensified when others decide to set boundaries or explain what their needs are, pointing out how different they are from the givers. In response the givers explode, withdraw, sulk, or cry, expressing how deeply hurt and angry they feel because their generosity has not been rewarded or appreciated. Instead they feel misunderstood.

The less worthy, loved, accepted, and appreciated they feel, the more likely they are to spiral into a state of desperation, trying to make things okay again. They will:

- Give gifts
- Write a lovely card
- Express how important and loved others are

It is all in an attempt to have the words spoken taken back or to remove the newly established boundaries that the lesson is experienced by the giver and the receiver. The unconscious motivation is to re-establish acceptance and approval for all actions taken, and that the receiver was wrong to reject the giver's generosity.

The Entangled Dance of Giver and Receiver

But the interaction goes further as the receiver recognises:

- The desperation to be loved in the giver
- How they have attached feelings and needs to the acts of kindness.
- The actions are what the giver wants done back to them

The giver is:

- Only able to identify their intent and helpfulness
- Attached to self-identity as being a helpful, nice, and lovable person

A compounding of resentment, frustration, and unspoken tension prevails. The receiver feels stifled, not wanting to burst the bubble by telling the giver the truth of how they experience them or the conditional giving. The giver stays stuck in their self-perception yet feels unappreciated. Silence traps both of them in a pattern of co-dependency, worthlessness, conditional giving, or service and acceptance of unhealthy relationships.

Co-dependence

In *Facing Co-dependency,* Pia Mellody states that co-dependants have trouble with being too dependent, being anti-dependent, being needless, and being wantless, or they get their wants and needs confused. A co-dependent who is needless, wantless, and anti-dependant will be reinforced when facing a co-dependent who is too dependent and confuses needs and wants. The giver and receiver become rigidified in their respective behaviours, feeding off and maintaining each other by being stuck in their corresponding patterns; this is the injustice perpetuating itself. It takes awareness and a change in behaviours, thinking, feeling, and actions to break out of this pattern.

Sympathising That Lacks Empathy

When interacting with others just so that they will focus on us, there is a lack of authenticity underlying the exchange because there is a lack of empathy for the other person's situation. This is covered over with words like, 'You poor thing. I'm so worried about you,' but the compassion is missing. There's no depth to the words. It's like it is being said from the intellect, with no heartfelt emotion attached.

In situations where it is only possible to feel for another by sympathising with them or feeling their pain as our own, we dramatically take over the situation and make it about us. Feeling hurt by the wrongdoing and then reacting melodramatically in an attempt to show just how loved the other person is doesn't meet the needs of the person actually going through the situation. Words and drama don't make them feel understood or loved. By projecting how we would feel if in the same situation and being engrossed in the wrongdoing, we forget to check with them if *they* are okay. We think our hyper-responses are telling them that we understand, care, and are concerned about their welfare. But these kinds of actions don't convey what is claimed to be known, and therefore it is only knowledge, not heartfelt knowledge, that influences our actions.

Debilitating Emotionality

When we are absorbed in the lesson of emotionality, we forget to process emotions and instead tend to wallow in emotional pain, looking for people to rescue us from our crisis. Convincing ourselves that strong people are all-knowing and wanting to be available to help with our healing traps us in patterns of injustice. Instead of learning and growing towards strength, we stay emancipated in powerlessness and victimhood, relying on others to fix, protect, and look after us. All this dense emotionality manifests in the human body as illness. It doesn't matter whether we are the giver or receiver—both end up exhausted by this imbalanced interaction.

Chronic fatigue and fibromyalgia are classic illnesses experienced in the lesson of emotionality. The only way they feel they can get their needs met is to be exhausted. The givers believe that if they aren't capable of doing anything for anyone else, then they will be given some attention. The receivers believe that if they are exhausted, others will drop their defences and come to their aide. This reinforces a pattern of illness and co-dependency. Whether we are anti-dependant or too dependent, we will manifest the same symptoms to deal with this out-of-control emotionality.

Hierarchy of Needs

Abraham Maslow's hierarchy of needs explores basic and advanced needs that influence our ability to achieve our full potential. The basic physiological needs are:

- Food
- Water
- Shelter
- Sex
- Safety
- Security

If these are not met, then we focus most of our attention on having them met on a day to day basis. For example, when coming from a poor, third-world country, one spends daily life earning money and sourcing food, water, and shelter to meet basic needs. When someone comes from a violent or abusive home, one's attention is on keeping safe and finding a sense of security in the environment; doing well at school becomes a secondary concern.

When living in countries free from war and physical threat, there is an opportunity to explore the higher needs:

- Self-esteem
- Belonging

- Love
- Truth
- Authenticity
- Justice
- Purpose

Maslow referred to the successful attainment of both basic and advanced needs as achieving self-actualisation. Pursuing the full expression of ourselves means wanting to:

- Be who we believe we really are
- Follow our dreams
- Manifest our destiny

It is also seeking:

- Justice and fairness in our personal lives and the external world
- Authenticity
- Honesty
- Truth
- Wholeness
- Adventure and fun
- Unity
- Self-knowledge

Ultimately we are all seekers of something, and so we seek to express all of who we are through our basic and higher needs.

Yet somehow life gets in the road. Fears lead us to think that others will not see or acknowledge our truth. We feel frustrated and impatient by the ordinariness of life. The daily grind doesn't feel intense enough, and we seek aliveness through dramatic experience.

The lesson of the injustice of emotionality is found in the need for intensity through emotional expression and experience. It runs on a continuum from obsessive and controlling behaviours to aloof, defensive, and cool mannerisms, to the child's temper tantrum, to power games snowballing, to hysteria and mental illness. The key is learning how to manage emotions through experiences. The challenge lies in a society that doesn't yet know how to be emotionally balanced. Parents, teachers, coaches, scout or guide leaders, religious leaders, politicians, and other authorities and role models display this lack of balanced emotionality on a daily basis, as reported in the news. Adults lacking the skills in emotional management can't teach children how to balance their emotions if they lack the skills themselves. The lesson of the injustice of emotionality is not just a personal journey but that of each family, culture, society, and nation.

The Snowball Effect

When observing the snowball effect, the person appears to be unreasonable, irrational, and illogical. The intensity of emotion appears disproportionate to the event, and it cannot be calmed or eased. Instead, any expression from the observer fuels snowballers' hysterical response. As they cry, rant, and rave about things, people, or events, it appears as if their memories are distorted. They remember events and conversations differently than others, and the details seem swapped around so that in their mind they were innocent and everyone else did wrong to them. All attempts to clarify actual facts will only lead to more attacks of blame, shame, and judgement, fuelling the hysteria of emotion.

When at the other end of snowballers' emotional explosion, people feel judged, misunderstood, blamed, punished, and condemned for what they did—and even for what they did not do. They feel as if they can do no right and that their needs don't matter, because snowballers must be appeased, and the dynamics of the relationship changes. As the relative, partner, friend, or colleague of snowballers, they:

- Become subservient and submissive
- Harbour resentment and hurt
- Remove themselves to avoid further attacks

Unfortunately, none of these responses will improve *snowballers'* emotionality because they don't experience the snowball effect in the same way as those who are at the receiving end.

The Snowballer Perspective

Snowballers perceive they are acting from what feels real to them. They do not believe their responses are extreme or unreasonable; they are simply trying to maintain a sense of self and self-worth. They are subconsciously driven by a deep and all-pervading fear of being unlovable, unacceptable, being disapproved of, and rejected, and a fear that their true self will be abandoned by those they love dominates their conscious thinking. The fear of being alone and not belonging pushes them to make everyone be the same. They are convinced that unity, togetherness, and closeness mean security, and they seek to know every detail in family and friends' lives because this gives a sense of connection. At the same time, they are certain that if everyone loves them as deeply as they love, then others will do everything possible to make them happy, including:

- Wearing what they want them to
- Doing what they want them to
- Thinking like they want them to
- Feeling in ways that they are comfortable with

As soon as others have their own opinions, personal style, attitudes, feelings, and thoughts, *snowballers* perceive rejection and fear abandonment. They are deeply hurt by such individuality, and emotional expression escalates as the perception of rejection and abandonment is all that is heard in others' words and all that is seen in their actions.

Snowballers need to be seen as perfect and right, otherwise their sense of self, persona, and self-image will crumble or shatter because they perceive others' actions as confirming their greatest, most personal fears: that they really aren't lovable or acceptable. They want these feelings to go away by making relatives, friends, family, partners, and colleagues behave in ways that make snowballers feel safe and secure, and that is all they know to maintain self-esteem.

After understanding what the snowball effect is driven by, whether the enactor of such emotionality or the receiver, it becomes possible to make choices about how to deal with such intense emotion and pain.

Snowballers can face their fears; take responsibility for thoughts, feelings, and actions; and heal wounds by loving, approving of, and accepting themselves as they are. By accepting that everyone is 'imperfectly perfect' and that through acceptance springs growth and change, they can work with the emotions to understand themselves and others rather than wielding emotions as a weapon.

The receiver of the snowball effect can express empathy and compassion for the pain by stepping out of the emotionality and acting and speaking from the heart. By telling snowballers that they love them and are okay just the way they are, they can take steps to break the intensity of the emotional expression. They begin to calm snowballers' fears and insecurities, and they have the power to act with love and to ease another's pain with kindness.

Emotional Intelligence

Through the lesson of emotionality, we will come to learn about emotions and their power and destructiveness. The concept of emotional intelligence is highly relevant to this lesson as so many of us think that if we feel emotional, that is being emotionally intelligent because we are strongly connected to our feeling world. Of course this is not the case at all, such as when we feel so emotional that we can't think our way through it, or we say whatever we think, or we act on our feelings and emotions immediately, or we feel so overwhelmed and swamped by our emotions that we are stuck in the emotionality. It is our ability to grow beyond this state that enables us to mature in emotional intelligence.

We can develop an ever evolving capacity to:

- Identify that we feel something about what is happening around us without acting on it immediately
- Thinking about what we say so that it reflects our highest truth
- Being responsible for our actions, thoughts, and feelings

- Knowing who we are in every moment and acting from this centre
- Holding ourselves accountable for what we say and do
- Being able to assess situations quickly and take action as necessary, drawing on both our logic and intuition

We will feel empowered by emotions rather than controlled by them. This allows us to expand awareness of not only ourselves but of others as we:

- Observe ourselves and our environment
- Become more self-aware and obtain a greater understanding of ourselves, and by extension others
- Recognise how everything is about choice and personal power
- Accept what is right now
- Develop and implement strategies to improve ourselves and any situation in which we find ourselves
- Know that if a situation cannot be changed, all we can change is our attitude towards it

This lifelong learning supports us to fully embrace emotional intelligence as we:

- Increase self-awareness and become more skilled at identifying our feelings
- Enhance how we develop our self-control as well as our ability to delay our need for gratification
- Learn to socialise in an appropriate manner
- Be able to motivate ourselves
- Have the ability to build our empathy for others
- Be appropriately optimistic
- Commit to noble goals

This approach empowers us to live in our truth and be authentic in who we are. It also permits us to know that this is an ever-evolving reality because each experience in life brings us into contact with parts of ourselves we may never have known before, and we enjoy the learning for what it is.

Living a Real Life

The lesson of the injustice of emotionality may provide the opportunity to see how we are moving through life without actually living it, because we are waiting for our real life to begin. Having had experiences that tore away innocence, we create the fantasy of another life waiting. There is no greater myth than the one about life-saving love. This lesson will connect into the archetypal myth of love. Movies, books, television, music, and computer games fill our minds with the myth that love will save us from our lives. The knight in shining armour always saves the wretched maiden—or as seen in Drew Barrymore's character in *Ever After*, the maiden now saves the wretched knight. Either way the message is clear: love makes the world go round, love lifts us up, and love is the answer. When we find love and our lives aren't miraculously transformed, we decide that:

- We aren't being loved enough
- We aren't loveable
- We aren't worthy of true love

We go in search for more.

A great freedom is available as we realise the lie in the myth. Love does not only come from a partner; we don't need to be loved by anyone for our real life to begin. Through this lesson, we have the opportunity to feel secure in the knowledge that this is our life. We are living it right now, and we are the only ones responsible for what happens in it. As adults, we no longer need to entrap ourselves in a child's pain of rejection, abandonment, or conditionality.

By looking back at our childhoods with empathy, compassion, and forgiveness, and by accepting the context of time and place, we can heal the sense of a lack of love from early caregivers. When we refuse to do this, we stay angry, bitter, and resentful of parents and extended family for their choices and circumstances. The longer we stay like this, the longer we stay in the myth of love fixing everything. Instead, relationships become complicated as we look to partners to be the ones to make up for the inadequacies of parents and families.

Life-saving Love

The lesson will provide us with an understanding of how the myth of life-saving love coming from another creates imbalances, because it disempowers the one who waits and burdens the one who saves, rescues, or helps the waitee. It prevents us from being the masters of our own destiny and promotes co-dependency. Romantic love is all about needing another to survive, becoming entangled in their lives, and merging feelings. The myth feeds into a sense of missing out when it isn't actualised and contributes to feelings of jealousy, envy, low self-worth, hurt, bitterness, resentment, hatred, and betrayal, as well as being unlovable, undeserving, and abandoned. It is a manufactured weakness in the human psyche.

Within us all lives the unconditionally loving heart that doesn't need rules to define how to be compassionate and empathic. If we can see the illusion, we will find a freedom that will strengthen our resolve, that enhances our resilience, and that allows growth and change. It is the freedom to be authentic and true to ourselves.

Wholeness through Parenthood

Generations of women were raised to believe that motherhood and the love of a baby would make them whole. This myth was perpetuated by a society that hated women and judged them as second-class citizens. Cultural conditioning has meant that women don't recognise they have absorbed the lie of worthlessness from the society. This aspect of the injustice of emotionality is found in women who resent being mothers. When raised in families who value boys above girls, they feel unworthy and unlovable. When told that a woman is only worthy of motherhood, they project their pain towards the child, labelling it as hard work and blaming it for being difficult to raise. In the meantime the child is just being a child, the teenager is just being a teenager, and the grown adult-child is just living their own life. Children are not bad or a burden or the problem—the sense of lack lies inside the mother. It is her sense of inadequacy that creates her perceptions, not the reality of the child.

If females have never been totally and completely loved and accepted just as they are, they are searching for what will take away the loneliness and fill their sense of lacking. This injustice is unfair to:

- The child, who has come to experience life for itself and doesn't need the burden of trying to make its mother's life okay
- The mother, because no child can or should make her feel lovable

- The husband, partner, or father, who never gets to be part of a healthy relationship because he is either cast in the role of sperm donor or rescuer

Being the focus of parents or caregivers seeking their pain and sense of lack to be healed by the child can be confusing, overwhelming, and daunting. If the children understand the context of the mother and accept that blaming and shaming her only leads to greater intensity of emotional hurt, the possibility to detach with love and understanding frees the adult-children from the injustice of such a burden.

Cultural Norms

Every country in the world has a common cultural norm about truth, fairness, and justice. In Australia, they equate the freedom of speech with the idea that a person is free to speak the truth. Australians aren't interested in lies spouted as the truth. They believe in a fair go and that individuals should always stick up for 'the little Aussie battler'. These attitudes reflect their concepts of truth, fairness, and justice, whereas in America the Bill of Rights supports the concept of the freedom to speak.

Philosophically, Americans pride themselves on protecting the rights of those who would destroy that which others fight to defend. Within this belief lies an awareness that resisting something doesn't make it go away. Transferring belief into action can be more challenging within the cultural setting, but this philosophy believes that people don't conquer things by killing them or filling others with fear. In fact, those very actions only create more fear and anger. Highly powerful emotions carry an energy that creates and attracts more of the same kind of energy and actions. Fear and anger allows people to feel justified in their stances as they voice a sense of righteousness and nobility in their behaviours. It is in the fight and struggle that suffering is maintained.

We are living in a current world environment where truth, fairness, and justice are being blurred by philosophical, religious, and cultural dogma. The lesson to be found in emotionality is that the more strongly we hold a point of view, the more strongly we believe we are right and that others are wrong; the more strongly we demand that others concede their flaws, their faults, and their wrongness; the more we maintain the status quo of hostility, misunderstanding, and violence in all its forms.

Rigidity stems from such intensity. The more strongly we hold rationalisations, the longer it will take to embrace the beauty in humanity. It is through truth, flexibility, allowing, and accepting that we all have the right to be whoever we are, providing it doesn't harm anyone else. Nothing changes when we are obsessively attached to outcomes or concepts of the way the world should be. It is through love that we find harmony and acceptance. It is the act of allowing that creates the possibility of infinite choice, and it is through choice that the power of love manifests itself.

Transformation

The transformation possible from the lesson of the injustice of emotionality will assist us to speak and act from the truth of our authentic self. By enjoying this experience and feeling stronger each time, we will begin to stop those things we do, say, or feel that are not a reflection of our real selves, but that are done from our own misconstrued ideas of love and belonging. We feel like we are in charge of our own lives, our real lives, the ones we are choosing to live right now, and we will become the masters of our destiny. Through setting clear and respectful boundaries within ourselves and others, the experience of proportional giving and receiving will be achieved. We no longer feel the need to explain or apologise for our truth, and we will share ourselves with others from a confident centre, able to perceive our reality and how others experience their own. By being able to be responsible for what we say, do, and think, we will bravely understand our impact on others and act with compassion and empathy. We will feel clear about who we are and where we are at. By stepping outside of the myths of love, we will find a great freedom to brightly shine our love of self.

CHAPTER 10

The Injustice of Injustice

'I reach beyond myself to see what I find, beyond
my mind. There is no time in this place beyond
my sight. My heart knows what is not yet
seen; I'm witnessing my own becoming.'
'Becoming', Jewel

THE LESSON OF THE INJUSTICE of injustice becomes conscious in our lives with the realisation that our existence creates someone else's injustice, just as others' existence creates our injustice. Embracing this possibility frees us from the need to judge, compare, compete, condemn, and punish others for being who they are. Life exposes all the shadow issues of wrath, envy, fear, hypocrisy, doubt, gluttony, greed, lust, sloth, pride, and deceit as we become aware of what we do to others, what others do to us, and what we do to ourselves. It is through an inability to process fears, insecurities, jealousies, and vulnerabilities that the experience of injustice is created.

We find our place of insufficiency through consciously accessing our hurt, sadness, anger, pain, and hope. Peeling away the layers to discover others inadequacies inspires us to dig deeper to ascertain the very foundations of societal lies and injustices that manifest as cultural insufficiency. The trauma created through inconsistent emotional development and the human need to minimise and justify wrongdoing as excusable will lead us through a complete re-evaluation of the meaning and purpose of our lives, as well as the choices available to be made from a place of consciousness.

Interpreting Injustice

Entering the world with a personality, genetic possibilities, and lessons to learn and grow through life initially covers over awareness and inner knowing. The accumulation of emotion about the unjust experiences tend to be suppressed, denied, and ignored because we are unable to integrate our child's perspective into our adult thinking. Children largely function from the right brain, which is the world of creative thought, imagination, and inventiveness. They are egocentric and relate the behaviours of others as being caused by something they have said or done.

Piaget's theory of cognitive development explains that as the brain moves into being concrete operational around the age of thirteen, we forget how we had previously perceived the world. We disconnect from our childhood understandings and function more from the left brain, intellectualising and rationalising experiences, which hinders the ability to process the entirety of our lives truthfully and with a balanced perspective because our perceptions are now coloured by our intellect.

Understanding the whys and wherefores of our lives is an important first step in the healing process. It is not that rational thought is bad or unnecessary, but thoughts and thinking are not feelings and emotion. Transforming our realities can be achieved by honouring feelings and processing experiences to identify, own, and integrate the hidden (or shadow) self. This allows an understanding of how we thought, felt, and acted as a child, and what interpretations were made of the events that occurred at that time, with who we now are as an adult.

All experiences, whether challenging and hurtful or loving and positive, make up who we are. Trying to separate the good from the bad gives power to the injustice, feeding the conscious mind with fears, doubts, and insecurities. These concerns contribute to feelings of vulnerability and a sense of lacking control. Integrating the duality in life allows for wholeness. Moving from attached absolutes of fairness and justice to an acceptance of what is integrated with the power of choice liberates us from the shackles of what is 'meant to be'. The freedom to give meaning and purpose to events in life becomes our choice.

Pain and Suffering as Lessons

How pain and suffering are expressed when experiencing injustice can be very challenging. There is often the original injustice sitting alongside the injustice created when other people deal inappropriately with our pain, our story, and our experiences. The lesson of the injustice of injustice enables us to begin to observe how our and others' inappropriate responses to injustice create and rigidify injustice.

Cultural conditioning creates expectations and formulates beliefs about injustice that feeds and maintains injustice. When we appear to have gotten over or survived any unfair or unjust events, we have to accept what happened at some level. Too often in accepting the injustice, we decide it was all right that it happened. For it to be all right, we must have deserved what happened, or wanted what happened, or needed what happened for our own good.

Children's minds decide they aren't good enough, are not worthy of being treated better, and have somehow failed or not got it right to deserve anything better. Every time we declare that we are who we are because of an unfair experience, we are solidifying the need for injustice to define who we are. This is not justice. It is how we have taken an external, unjust event and internalised the interpretation of why it has happened to us. This is how we move from being a victim of someone else's unfair behaviour to victimising ourselves by justifying that we deserved it.

We often become petty and underhanded towards those we feel hurt by, and we justify our actions by pointing the finger at others. At other times we will treat another person how we were treated, because we recognise a quality within them that was once how we were. This pattern will continue until we face that the unfair and unjust behaviour is not acceptable no matter who does it, even us.

We also learn from positive experiences, but because they are enjoyable, we place little value on them. By becoming more conscious, we can choose to evolve and grow through experiencing ourselves as the best we can be. It takes a lot of courage to shine brightly; it brings with it opportunities to explore our sense of worth and our capacity for self-love and self-respect. Gaining greater and greater expressions of ourselves through deeper and deeper levels of self-acceptance takes us on a journey filled with surprises, excitement, and adventure.

Connecting to Intuition

When experiencing the lesson of injustice, we will want to name the injustice for what it is. Knowing there is no justifiable reason for someone else's inappropriate behaviour and accepting reasons only adds to the injustice. An opportunity to shift paradigms opens up new ways to understand and interact with others.

Realising that there is a time to act and a time to be silent learning to hear our inner voice assists in deciding on what is the best course of action to take to break the patterns of injustice. The challenge is recognising the difference between our minds' negative self-talk, the mental chatter, and our intuition. But recognise it we must. To find our truth, we must peel off the layers of messages that have accumulated over a lifetime, and we must hear our inner guidance. Where we feel locked into our sense of inadequacy, we will find it harder to hear our intuition.

Insufficiency Mentality

The insufficiency mentality occurs when feeling inadequate, not good enough, and as if we are personally lacking something within ourselves. When the outer world acts in ways that don't validate who we are or our worth, and we internalise judgements, words, or actions to feel worthless and unlovable, then we are coming from a place of insufficiency. Believing we are inadequate, we interact with the world through a filter of insufficiency. This is why the ultimate injustice of injustice is that we don't see how wonderful we are. We are unable to stay connected to this truth and seek others to validate us—and when they don't, we spiral into states of dependency, helplessness, powerlessness, confusion, and indecisiveness. We feel like victims to life.

There are many perspectives formed from the insufficiency mentality.

Insufficiency Mentality Perspective #1: Specialness

If we have a strong sense of self and feeling special, we want attention, to be spoilt and fussed over, and to have our needs and wants met how we desire. By looking to the outer world to validate this with positive reassuring, affirming words, and actions, we react strongly to the slightest negative experience with a sense of rejection, abandonment, and worthlessness, and by feeling unloved.

Insufficiency Mentality Perspective #2: Dependency

We prefer someone else to take care of us—not because we can't, but because we don't want to—and this becomes an issue of what we deserve, not of responsibility. By having the aptitude to recognise people's abilities and avail them, we see only how it benefits everyone involved. We have no difficulty asking for help because we have a belief system that says people will help us, people want to help us, and we deserve people helping us. We feel incredibly hurt when our requests are denied.

The pattern of dependency can be created from a family where:

- The parents loved to do everything for their children. They didn't teach the life skills needed to be independent because they liked to be needed. This explains why we believe people enjoy doing things for us because our parents did.
- The parents abdicated their responsibilities, and we became the parent. We resent this burden of responsibility and think it's our right to be taken care of, to compensate for our childhood experiences.

- The parents lacked productive self-care skills themselves, being unable to role model healthy self-management and self-control, and they behaved erratically. We now imitate this chaos and, when held accountable, revert to wanting others to take care of our needs and wants rather than learning skills to enhance our own lives.

Insufficiency Mentality Perspective #3: Helplessness

By believing it is our birthright to be helped and to say no, we don't do anything we don't want to. When push comes to shove, we can be very strong and assertive and appear to have no qualms about standing up for ourselves and getting what we need or want. Likewise, we expect others to ask for their needs to be met and that everyone is only doing things they want to do. When this reality is challenged, helplessness ensues to avoid the impact we may be having on others. Instead, we turn the tables and project the injustice, questioning motives and intentions of actions. We feel abandoned, discarded, and rejected by others' behaviours, and we make sure everyone knows the sacrifice or inconvenience that a situation has been to us.

Insufficiency Mentality Perspective #4: Powerlessness

Despite believing that we are worth acting for, our personal power to act on our own behalf has been riddled with inconsistent results. We are not able to make people act exactly how we want, and we have plunged into a sense of powerlessness that blinds us from our true nature. Denying our strength, assertiveness, and skills prompts us to interact with the world, compounding injustices and our sense of powerlessness. We feel incapable of changing our circumstances and miss the links between thoughts, actions, intentions, and outcomes. We don't associate our words or behaviours with the responses or actions from others. By never learning how to build our emotional muscle and how to become resilient when held accountable for our actions, we don't step up but sulk and feel wronged, coagulating our powerlessness.

Insufficiency Mentality Perspective #5: Confusion

When we know that we are innately special, lovable, and worthy—but we experience a world that doesn't act as if this is true—confusion replaces security and surety. Relationships become complicated because there is a mutual struggle to understand each other. By believing that all hurt and confusion could be resolved if only others could walk in our shoes and see the world though our eyes, we feel more isolated and misunderstood when this is not achieved. Sabotaging our own lives to gain the attention, sympathy, and love of others further traps us in our sense of helplessness, powerlessness, and co-dependency. When in isolation, we are convinced no one understands us, we are perplexed by responses from those we seek love and approval from, and our emotional pain intensifies. Confusion reigns as we think others need to be more considerate and responsible towards us, and yet they claim it is we who need to be more considerate and responsible. Their existence creates our injustice just as our existence creates theirs, and our sense of inadequacy spirals into insufficiency thinking.

Insufficiency Mentality Perspective #6: Indecisiveness

When we innately believe in our capacity to manifest all we dream of, life begins to contradict desire from reality.

By submerging into our sense of helplessness, powerlessness, and co-dependency, we reluctantly accept that we can't have everything we want. Now all we can do is pick one thing; we can only put our time, effort, and energy into one aspect of life. Picking between success in work, family, friends, sport, hobbies, and recreation makes us reason that we have finite skills. We don't want to spread those skills too thinly and display maturity by making a choice about what we can have. We're not aware of the limitations and injustice being created, and we respond erratically to others' responses to our choices. By swinging from full dedication to the option selected to plunging into despair, worry, and angst over what had to be given up, we sabotage the current choice, believing that we chose incorrectly. When we're cycling through this process, indecision paralyses us in a rut of never achieving our goals.

Insufficiency Mentality Perspective #7: Victimhood

When we're attuned to a sense of self that is innocent of any wrongdoing or harm, and we strongly identify with our wounds, traumas, and hurts, the emotional pain is so intense that we feel victimised by it, crippling us from being able to face the impact we might have on others. We prefer not to be told, held accountable, or asked to validate others in their experiences of us. By connecting into how fragile, vulnerable, and weak we feel, we believe there is a need to be protected from the reality of the complexity of human relationships.

Where natural laws, rules, and cultural customs have implied and actual consequences, we will distort the events to ensure we remain the victim. We align ourselves with others who are

erable, weak, and powerless. This enables us
ours. Ultimately we haven't learnt how to
...perfection, and instead guilt and shame
...t away from any source of accountability. It is
...y for us to fall into self-pity because we genuinely
...nsider it as terrible when things happen to us.

Experiencing Someone with an Insufficiency Mentality

An insufficiency mentality leads to a struggle in considering all the influencing factors and human dynamics that are entwined into personal, intimate, or professional relationships. When dealing with someone who has an insufficiency mentality, it is common to consider the person as:

- A hypocrite, liar, and selfish
- Thinking in illogical and irrational terms
- Refusing to be held accountable and not liking consequences
- Having personality qualities that are offensive
- Intentionally refusing to use skills, strength, abilities, talents, and gifts
- Refusing to express appreciation or gratitude

When feeling betrayed, tricked, used, and exploited for being nice, caring, and thoughtful—or as if the one with an insufficient mentality has given up on the relationship or interaction by either not picking to put in sufficient time, energy, and effort or not using their skills to improve a situation themselves the partner, friend, or colleague—is left exhausted, drained, and depleted.

Insufficiency Creates Injustice

To make sense of others, we will find ourselves battling our belief system to find universal truths that bring understanding and compassion to our daily interactions. We look for how we are a reflection of each other, and we will turn to the concept of 'proportional response', the degree to which we feel something is reflected in the intensity expressed in our behaviours. If proportional response is applied to those with an insufficient mentality, we will see that they are expressing external rigidity to the degree to which they feel insecure or insufficient on the inside. The very fears they are strongly attached to make life feel hard and inflexible, as if their needs can't be met. It sucks the joy and fun out of life and dries up passion and creativity. It makes us sad and can make us angry, even spiteful, revengeful, and vindictive. It feels like life has no place of fairness, justice, or equality. It maintains rules and limitations. It leads us to seek substitutes for love and belonging in food, alcohol, shopping, and other addictions. It feeds into greed and gluttony and supports a slothful approach to life. It ultimately makes us all hypocrites as we struggle to live a life of integrity and congruency. Who we are on the inside isn't expressed on the outside because of the limitations created in all this lack.

Emotional Development

Everyone is likely to have an area of insufficiency. Robin Grille explores the five rites of passage of core emotional development in his book *Parenting for a Peaceful World,* and it is in one or several of these rites that we will find from where the insufficiency stems. The more stages missed, the more insufficient we will feel.

The first rite of passage is the right to exist, and it begins from conception and goes until around six months of age. The key issues at this time are about being wanted, feeling connected to parents, feeling safe, and being worthy just because we were born. The beliefs formed at this time reflect our experiences, perceptions, and interpretations of how parents were feeling during this phase. Where we feel their love and acceptance, our brain neurons connect in ways that support us to feel loved, worthy, safe, and connected.

When we feel their stress and worry, their fears and doubts, and even their regret and disappointment about our presence in their lives, our brain neurons connect in ways that make us focus on the need to survive because the world will feel dangerous and threatening. When feeling this deep sense of aloneness and isolation, we feel like there is something innately wrong with us and that we don't have the right to take up space or be here.

The second rite of passage is the right to need; this begins from birth and lasts until about eighteen months of age. The key issues here are: Am I allowed to have needs, and will they be met? When the only form of communication is through crying, we learn from parents' responses to our cries of need about the right to have needs and whether we will have them met. Where we were picked up and reassured by a calm and loving parent who learnt to read the different cries, we absorb the message that we can have needs and that they will be met appropriately. We learn how we can be nourished by life and believe in abundance.

Where we are left to cry beyond natural time responses, we are not held while being fed, and eye contact and physical touch is limited, we experience the world as dangerous and isolating. The brain neurons connect in ways that focus on keeping ourselves safe because we feel abandoned and alone. We learn that it is safer to not want anything from anyone, and instead we must meet all of our needs and wants. The focus shifts from someone looking after us to the awareness that to be safe we must please others, be aware of others, and make them happy at all times if we are to survive. By extension we will feel like we are unlovable and undeserving of love or of having any of our needs met.

The third rite of passage is the right to have support; this begins around the age of ten months and continues until the age of two years. The key issues here are learning to trust that others will support us, that we can ask for help and receive it as well as feeling safe in expressing our vulnerability, strength, and independence. Where adults support us in the early attempts of crawling, walking, and talking with words of encouragement, gentleness, acceptance of our mistakes, failed attempts and mishaps, we will develop a deep sense of ourselves as being lovable just the way we are. This sense will extend into our confidence to give things a go and our willingness to take risks to learn new skills, because we will feel supported and strong within our vulnerabilities.

Where we are shamed, humiliated, punished, and limited in our freedom to try things, we feel unsupported and shamed for who we are. We learn that we can't trust anyone and feel we can never let anyone see our vulnerabilities, weaknesses, and failings. We become suspicious of others motives and learn to survive by manipulating ourselves and others to always keep our most vulnerable self safe. Through this, the lessons of the injustice of deception, temptation, and limitations become major themes in our lives.

The fourth rite of passage is the right to freedom. This begins around the age of two and continues until we are four. The key themes here revolve around our ability to separate from our mother and form the first concepts of ourselves as a different and unique person from that of parents and extended family members. This is a time to learn about balance as we discover our flow and rhythm. We learn about relationships and conflict management as we express our own opinion and demand our needs be met and how they have to be balanced with others needs and opinions.

Where parents embrace our fledging independence and personal power, we learn to be creative, self-expressive, and comfortable in finding and developing our unique sense of self. We learn that it is okay to be autonomous and make decisions for ourselves, and that we have the right to our personal space, dignity, and privacy. We learn to approve of ourselves even when others don't.

Where we are bound by rules and restriction, we internalise these as life being filled with struggle and suffering, and love being accompanied with duty and obligations. We feel overwhelmed by the *shoulds* of life and begin to believe that if we are to be free, we will be alone and isolated. We will feel trapped by the expectations of others.

The fifth rite of passage is the right to love; this begins around the age of three and continues until six or seven. The key themes here are around the ability to embrace and enjoy pleasure in life, and around our capacity to feel love for others and receive love from another. A great deal of adult behaviours in relationships develops from experiences during this time. It is during this stage that we are in love with our opposite gender parent and compete for their attention from our same-sex parent. How we are treated by this parent prepares us for what we accept and expect from our intimate adult relationships.

Where our parent embraces our attention, spends valuable time with us, and expresses their love openly, gently, and lovingly, we will grow up believing in our right to be loved and treated with respect and honesty for all of whom we are. Likewise, we will have the capacity to love with our whole being and look for a partner who will reciprocate this back. We will be able to embrace pleasure and joy in life and know that we are lovable for ourselves not what we do or have to offer another.

Where our attempts for attention are repelled, we will feel unlovable and not good enough for others. We will have distorted perceptions about intimacy, and our sexual self will be tainted with guilt and rejection.

From the children's perspective, when they experience not having an emotional need met at any of these phases, it creates a trauma in their brain development, resulting in neurons connecting differently to those who received their emotional needs. This connection influences the degree to which they experience insufficiency, how adaptable they become, and their perception that there is not enough. As they integrate their physiological development with genetic, personality and on-going life lessons a manufactured reality is created. As adults bringing people into our lives to mirror what rites of passage haven't yet been healed, resolved or have been suppressed into the shadow self makes life looks as if reality is the truth.

Understanding how the brain develops can help explain why there are different memories and interpretations of events according to the age we were when things occurred in our lives. Each of these rites of passage will play out in our lives for a second time during our adolescence and again in adulthood. To be human is to seek the experience of knowing our rights to exist, need, have support, be free, and love. The lesson of the injustice of injustice contaminates our ability to process our reality as we become trapped by society's lies that we cannot hold others accountable for their impact on us, because they couldn't help it or were doing their best at the time. Although this is true, it doesn't preclude us from feeling our pain, and through accepting this, we will transform into the best self we can be.

The Reciprocation of Injustice

The more tightly beliefs are held, the greater the possibility that interactions with those holding opposing views will occur. Like a magnet is attracted to its contrasting energy, we are bound to be mutually attracted to our opposite. The yin and yang of life: one exists because of the other. Without the other, we have no context in which to place our experiences. Coming to the awareness that our existence creates injustice for another just as their existence creates injustice for us transforms our personal paradigm.

An example would be the interaction between a person who believed in the value of delaying gratification and a person who sought instant gratification.

In emotional intelligence theory, delayed gratification is a prized natural quality to be born with. With a worldview about patience, process, work, responsibility, and sharing, they accept the time it takes for goals to be achieved. The time it takes confirms that being patient and working hard towards objectives ratifies how the world works.

Meeting people who believe in instant gratification—and who appear to get what they want quickly and without much effort—challenges beliefs about reality. It doesn't seem fair that they get what they want without working hard and being patient. Their ability for instant gratification gives them their capacity for instant manifestation. To manifest dreams, we have to be willing to receive what is available immediately. Those who have the ability for instant gratification-manifestation are open to receive opportunities. This challenges the worldview of those who believe in delaying gratification.

But it's not all smooth sailing for those who can manifest quickly due to their ability to receive instant gratification. When experiencing sensitivity in the ability to create in the world, they are challenged by their capacity to manifest negative thoughts and feelings just as quickly as they manifest positive ones. The power to create what is thought is often overwhelming. By trying to separate from the effects produced, they convince themselves that they are victims of circumstance, not the creators of their realities. Fear is often manifested with great drama and heightened awareness. They watch those who believe in delayed gratification have fears, and they don't manifest instantly. This seems unfair and challenges those with the capacity for instant gratification. In this interplay of desire, longing, and truth-seeking, each person represents the experience of injustice for the other.

Opposites have the potential to create experiences of injustice, including:

- A just world versus injustice
- An abundance mentality versus a scarcity mentality
- Responsibility versus irresponsibility
- Choice versus no choice
- Flexibility versus rigidity
- Growth and change versus stagnation and procrastination

The purpose of the lesson of the injustice of injustice is to comprehend the ways in which rigid thinking, both positive and negative, creates injustice for someone. The injustice lays in the attachment to a situation, a person, an emotion, an expectation, or a belief. Freedom and balance come through the realisation that life is about preferred ways of being and through learning to become more resilient when things aren't the way we want, all while working towards improving each situation to the best of our ability.

Timing

Through the lesson of the injustice of injustice, we have an awareness of our sense of timing and of our capacity for being ready for what life presents. Often major events occur when we aren't ready to receive them, or because they happen according to someone else's need or timing, which contributes to feeling like our lives never reflects us.

By the time we are conscious that there was an opportunity available to us, it has passed. We regret the missed opportunity and try to follow the signs to be ready for the next chance. Our enthusiasm can trap us into making whatever appears next in our life be what we want, or we justify it as what is *meant to be* in an attempt to prove we can receive opportunities. In reality we are never present in the now! We are always looking to the future for what a situation *might* mean, and we react to the past, trying to heal and learn from it. The more pain stored in our unconscious minds, the more our current lives will look like our pasts as we continue to re-enact our beliefs over and over again.

Relationships often reflect the capacity for timing and readiness. We frequently treat the current partner based on what we experienced in our previous relationship. Projecting our unresolved issues onto this current partner complicates the relationship when our perception does not reflect who they are or what they have said or done. We balk at being treated poorly or wrongly accused, and we are left confused, shocked, and hurt when the other person chooses to end the relationship.

Based upon that experience, we then decide what we will do in our next relationship. We haven't met the next partner yet, but we have already pre-determined how we will behave in that relationship. This reactionary process is filled with insufficiency. By mistrusting ourselves and others by assuming how they will treat us, we will have a series of unsatisfying relationships. When we consciously stop this pattern, we are able to greet partners with no expectations as to who they are and what they will do in a relationship. Being present to feelings as they arise and owning the triggers clarity enables us to experience relationships in a new light. From a place of strength, we can act from integrity and not fear to make choices about the relationship and its suitability for us.

Micro-Macro Theory

Through the lesson of the injustice of injustice, we will explore the concept of micro-macro theory: the individual creates the society, and the society creates the reality of the individual. Injustice occurs when there is separation and disconnection between the individual and the society, culture, environment, and global family. Heartmath's™ research shows the links between individual actions and the state of the world at large. Upon reaching a level of consciousness and opening up to the possibility that *we are all one,* that the planets' existence and our global responsibilities are also our personal responsibilities, we see the connection between what we think and what is created.

Quantum physics is exploring and explaining an energetic world that is exhilarating, daunting, mind-expanding, and obvious. The inherent injustice that lays in the scientific mind-set of the mechanistic nature of mankind limits the full experience of a human life. Whether we call it our soul, our spirit, or our energetic body through meridians and chakras, the truth is that our emotional, mental, spiritual, and physical functioning are entwined.

Candace Pert, in her book *Molecules of Emotion,* opened the door to understanding our emotions as physical peptide molecules that lock into cells' receptor sites, activating physical responses to our emotional feelings. Norman Doidge's book *The Brain That Changes Itself* explores neuroplasticity and how the brain continues to form and reform itself in relation to our life experiences. Caroline Myss in *The Anatomy of the Spirit* presents the concept of how our biographies become our biology. In other words, what we feel, think, and experience becomes locked into the physical body and forms the cellular memory. Our physical bodies then look like what we have experienced.

These discoveries can liberate us to find the connection we seek to ourselves and to everyone and everything else in the world. If we identify our capacity to be like everyone, the tendency to judge and condemn others will lose its power. By developing compassion and empathy for every living form, we move towards a place of acceptance and understanding. The desire for tolerance, unity, and wholeness will override the social conditioning of comparison, competition, and winning. We see people as *people* rather than idolised images of perfection and come to understand the true meaning of equality, freedom, and personal power. We will live in a time of choice.

Right and Wrong

Western capitalist society has moved from one that simply denies overt injustice even exists to now trying to justify injustice in an attempt to accept it. The very moral fibre of the social structure is in question when we:

- Allow wrong action to be right in certain circumstances
- Excuse actions due to the past experiences of the wrongdoer
- Justify that it must be okay because everyone does it

Trying to find common values that can define right from wrong is the challenge of every generation. Compounding this modern dilemma is the human resistance to concepts of responsibility and choice. It is evident when listening to world leaders trying to justify everything from war to sexual indiscretions. Injustice prevails every time an individual tries to avoid being responsible for thoughts, words, feelings, deeds, and actions. By refusing to be conscious of our personal, social, and global responsibility, and by declining to hold others accountable for irresponsibility, we are denying the power of choice and free will. Inaction is still a choice. We have a responsibility to make wise, informed, and loving choices if we truly want a fair, humane, and just society.

Correcting Past Injustices

We live in a time where many injustices of the past are being confronted. For example, we are no longer accepting situations or staying ignorant to the impact of abuse on children. When the scientific model of disease is applied to the social-emotional paradigm of relationships and family dynamics, eliminating or eradicating injustice becomes far more complicated. As we begin to explore the complexity of energy exchange and how unresolved issues form a charge that vibrates and attracts more of the same, society will stop seeking simplistic solutions to complicated, multifaceted problems.

Family therapist Bert Hellinger examines the concept of forgiveness and injustice. When one simply forgives someone for hurtful actions without there being an action that re-balances the relationship, the act of forgiveness now creates an injustice that has to be compensated. The wronged person becomes innocent and superior to the guilty one. What tends to happen is that the only way to absolve the sense of guilt is to do something worse. True justice can only exist when there has been a compensatory exchange. There is a need to equalise the injustices experienced to allow balance to return. In human interactions there is never a void, a nothingness, an empty space when a wrong is named. New dynamics are formed, and with it new family, cultural, or societal patterns. We don't just break a pattern or disclose secrets, and then have balance restored. Change and transformation take effort, work, and sincerity to equalise injustice.

Creating Injustice through Illogical Thinking

Illogical thinking is where:

- We don't think there *are* any consequences to our choices
- We don't think there *should be* any consequences for our choices
- We want to be rewarded for our choices, behaviours, and actions even if they create less desirable results

Examples of illogical thinking occur:

- When we think we should be able to eat what we want, do no exercise, and yet weigh our ideal weight

- When we think yelling, name calling, and putting down our children will do no harm to their self-worth and self-esteem
- When we think we can do all the things that cause a heart attack or diabetes or cancer but won't get any of these diseases
- When we think we deserve something extra and free when we have caused the problem
- When we think we have rights and refuse to act with any sense of responsibility about those rights
- When we think it's acceptable to activate our rights even if it denies someone else's privacy and dignity

Let's look at an example. Say we have been in a car accident and smashed the car; it has to be taken to the panel beaters to be fixed. They tell us it will cost a certain price, and they need the car for five days. This is an inconvenience to us, though we forget that it was we who had the car accident. We ask the panel beater what extra jobs they are going to do to compensate us for having our car for so many days. This illogical perspective stems from the belief that we are doing *them* a favour, and so they owe us something for having our car to work on. We cannot use the car for five days and so believe we should receive something extra. We had the car accident, however, and not having the car for five days while it is fixed is the natural consequences of our actions. Not accepting this creates injustice for others.

Cultural Insufficiency

As we evolve through the lesson of the injustice of injustice, we come to examine how society creates, maintains, and encourages beliefs, attitudes, values, expectations, and desires that form our collective injustice. Every culture has them. The American dream that people can live harmoniously together with diverse and opposing opinions is a great example. Imagine living in a world where:

- People who believed that Jews were vermin to be killed were able to live next to a Jew and not act on that belief
- White people who believed they were superior to black people, who were to be owned and controlled by them, and not act on it
- People arrive on a continent and believe it to be an empty land because of the absence of permanent buildings, and then they don't declare it to belong to them

But none of these are reflected in human actions.

The preamble of the Australian constitution still has Australia as 'terra nullius', an empty land, denying the indigenous population who lived there for 60,000 years. America had slaves, and the Nazis exterminated millions of Jews in World War II. Our values and beliefs influence our attitudes, behaviours, and actions. Philosophically, it would be ideal to have diverse views and live happily side by side, but the reality is that it is more complicated than that because we act on our values and beliefs.

The denial of the injustice created by cultural beliefs compounds the experience of injustice for those victimised by those beliefs. By refusing to take responsibility for the impact of cultural values and beliefs, society tries to justify injustice and make it excusable. The entire point of something being an injustice is that it is unfair. The denial tends to lead to more rigidity, dogma, fanaticism, extremism, and hatred, with violence and brutality winning out over love, peace, harmony, and tolerance.

Disentangle Ourselves

Life is unfair and unjust. The structure of a patriarchal society with winners and losers is an unjust system full of opposites that presents a vision of the world that is *how it is meant to be*. Ideas such as being perfect, good enough, and deserving are the myths of society that create the injustice of injustice. Fighting against any societal system only sees it continue and sometimes become stronger. Reform that educates and empowers can bring lasting change. The same applies to the individuals that make up that society.

Children form ideas about themselves in an attempt to make them feel okay about whom they are. Once we are adults, it is our responsibility to make ourselves okay. In fact it could be the very purpose of our lives: to disentangle ourselves from the limitations, perceptions, interpretations, and beliefs created in response to the events that have been our life.

By moving into a place of acceptance with how life is, we can engage life and others free of judgement, expectations, and condemnation. Jealousy and envy, which lead to the punishment of others, becomes pointless. Accepting diversity and difference opens us to the recognition of personal choice. As we come from a place of peace, love, service, and wisdom, we will know that we can only be free and equal by allowing others to be free and equal.

We can revolutionise the concept of 'things being bad enough', and we can redefine the acceptance of abuse, intolerance, and prejudice. Rather than grading abuse and violation, a standard of living that protects the innocent will warrant action and acknowledgement of the injustice. While moving beyond the personalisation of life and transcending the limitations of society, we will make sense of the insensible. Our journey is to step out of the illusion, and by example we will shine our light into the dark that allows everyone to be liberated, if that is their choosing. We will set ourselves free to thrive.

Transformation

The transformation possible from the lesson of the injustice of injustice occurs when we connect into personal truth and access the ability to act from a place of integrity. We will challenge, expand, and engage our daily life with a purity of gratitude, enthusiasm, and passion. When we know that we are of equal worth to everyone no matter one's role or position in this world, we will want to treat others with the respect and honour that they deserve. The ability to live with our vulnerability as our strength will enable us to fully feel reality.

The challenge of finding and maintaining balance in a world that wants to distort authenticity will provide ample opportunities for us to learn about ourselves and others. As we do this, we will disentangle ourselves from injustice and begin to find others travelling this journey. Together we will work towards sending our inner peace, harmony, love, service, and wisdom out into the world matrix. As we heal our hurts, wounds, and traumas, we will heal the burdens of the world psyche, allowing for a collective transformation of consciousness. By working beyond the limitations of personal, cultural, and global beliefs, we will come to find the ability to expand is unending, exciting, and enjoyable when it feeds the best in us, others, and the world at large. We are all one.

CHAPTER 11

We Are All Onions

CREATING A DAILY PRACTICE OF self-care enables you to consciously process your life experiences and to grow into who you already are. To quote Shrek and expand his self-declaration, we are all onions, not just ogres, and as such you need to peel away your layers to uncover your true self—who you were born to be. The muck that has covered over your connection to your core self slows down your processing and fills up the space in between your experiences as you try to make sense of the insensible.

The four self-care techniques I recommend to you are journal writing, taking flower essences as part of your life journey, using emotional freedom technique on a daily basis, and matrix reimprinting for deeper transformation of life's lessons.

Journal Writing

By writing in a journal each day, we will become more conscious of our thoughts, feelings, and intuition. To help work through each injustice, the following process in writing is helpful.

- Begin by writing what the issue is
- Start detailing the facts: who is involved, what was said, the looks on faces, the tone in the voice, the body positions and postures
- Now reflect on how you felt about it all
- Identify what you wanted from the interaction and what your needs were
- What did you learn about yourself and others? Assess if this is the most positive perspective you can have, and ask whether it will increase harmony, peace, love, and wisdom for all involved
- What is the outcome going to look, sound, and feel like for you now? How are you going to feel, think, and act? Detail how you will treat yourself and interact with others in general, specifically those involved in this situation

To help you dissect your experiences as well as add depth to the situations, consider the following aspects of everyone involved:

What basic needs are being desired in your situation?

Worth	Achievement	Support	Money
Belonging	Safety	Acceptance	Security
Importance	Respect	Love	Adequacy
Approval	Nurturing	Desirability	Wholeness
Esteem	Recognition	Validation	Freedom

What emotions are being expressed by you and those involved?

Loss	Happiness	Insecurity	Fear
Grief	Anger	Worry	Sadness
Joy	Confusion	Doubt	Shame
Pride	Anxiety	Hopelessness	Pity
Delight	Bitterness	Gratitude	Irritation
Frustration	Amusement	Abandonment	Hostility
Ecstasy	Self-satisfaction	Appreciation	Excitement
Anticipation	Disappointment	Longing	Angst

What are motivating the behaviours of everyone involved, including you?

Success	Recognition	Approval	Love
Acceptance	Obligation	Pressure	Friendship
Help others	Security	Achievement	Winning
Accomplishment	Possessions	Pleasure	Freedom
The challenge	Duty	Control	Revenge

Non-verbal language communicates louder than the words you speak. Your mind takes in both verbal and non-verbal data when assessing any situation. When observing others, you need to create a starting base of mannerisms, behaviours, and features, comparing these to the changes observed during an interaction without making judgements or assumptions of what they mean.

What to Observe

1. Body posture, generally
2. Hands and feet—positions and movements

3. Skin—colour, tightness
4. Mouth and nose—movements, tightness, colour
5. Eyes—contact pattern, expressiveness, moisture
6. Vocal expressiveness—pitch, tone, volume, intensity, flow
7. Breathing patterns—shallow, laboured, deep sighing
8. Gestures—movement of arms, hands, and body with particular words and expressions
9. Facial expressions—frown, smile, troubled

The more constructive your observation of people becomes, the more you will be able to turn the skill inwardly to learn to observe your own body language and the changes that occur during interactions. You can then include these observations in your journal writing as well. This will help you be congruent in words and body language. It will also help you communicate and clarify with others what they say with how they appear.

Flower Essences

Flower essences are the liquid essence of the particular flower from which it has been made. They are generally taken orally in a mix but can be used as a spray to help transform negative emotions, feelings, and thoughts into positive expressions that are true to our inner nature. There are many different companies worldwide that make flower essences, but the most widely known is Bach from England. Others include:

- America: Flower Essence Society, Desert Alchemy, Tree Frog Farm, Spirit-in-Nature, Alaskan
- Asia: Flora of Asia
- Australia: Australian Bush, Living Essences

- Brazil: Essênias Florais
- New Zealand: First Light
- Scotland: Findhorn
- South Africa: South African Flower Essences

A mix of essences is taken each day in a dosage of eight drops twice daily for about twenty-five days. Flower essences are a wonderful inclusion in your daily self-care practice, but you will need to access a practitioner to make up relevant mixes for you. As a guide, the following mixes are the sprays I've created that relate to each of the injustices:

The Injustice of Idleness Flower Essence Mix: Flower Essence Society essences: Mountain Pride, Penstemon; Living Essences: Illyarrie, Geraldton Wax, Shy Blue Orchid, Swan River Myrtle and White Eremophila

Purpose of the mix: Assists you in building emotional muscle by feeling strong within and having clarity about the events in your life.

The Injustice of Hypocrisy Flower Essence Mix: Australian Bush essence: Billy Goat Plum; Bach essence: Beech; Flower Essence Society essences: Angelica and Mullein; Living Essences: Fuchsia Grevillea

Purpose of the mix: Assists you in being more congruent between what you think and what you say and do.

The Injustice of Deception Flower Essence Mix: Desert Alchemy essences: Cardon Cactus and Mariola; Flower Essence Society essences: Calendula, Deerbrush, and Mullein

215

Purpose of the mix: Assists you in aligning to your inner truth, embracing your shadow self, and communicating with clarity.

The Injustice of Limitations Flower Essence Mix: Bach essences: Chestnut bud, Impatiens, and Water Violet; Desert Alchemy essence: Teddy Bear Cholla Cactus; Flower Essence Society essence: Goldenrod

Purpose of the mix: Assists you in balancing your engagement with the outer world and calming you to ensure the learning of lessons as they unfold.

The Injustice of Temptation Flower Essence Mix: Australian Bush essence: Fringed Violet; Bach essence: Star of Bethlehem; Flower Essence Society essences: Canyon Dudleya, Pink Monkeyflower, and Sticky Monkeyflower

Purpose of the mix: Assists you in forming healthy sexual boundaries and self-respect by releasing shame and restoring clarity and calmness.

The Injustice of Selfishness Flower Essence Mix: Australian Bush essences: Bluebell and Southern Cross; Desert Alchemy essences: Crown of Thorns and Desert Sumac; Flower Essence Society essences: Star Thistle and Trillium

Purpose of the mix: Assists you in clearing a fear of lack and embracing a sense of abundance.

The Injustice of Vanity Flower Essence Mix: Bach essence: Cerato; Flower Essence Society essences: Iris, Pink

Yarrow, and Sunflower; Living Essences e
Glory Grevillea

Purpose of the mix: Assists you to unify your
emotional boundaries and balancing your sense of self (ego).

The Injustice of Intimidation Flower Essence Mix: Bach
essence: Chicory; Flower Essence Society essences: Chaparral
and Mountain Pennyroyal; Living Essences: Cape Bluebell,
Swan River Myrtle, and White Eremophila

Purpose of the mix: Assists you to unlock deep hurt depicted
as anger, step out of using emotions to justify behaviours, and
transform how you relate to others.

The Injustice of Emotionality Flower Essence Mix: Bach
essence: Honeysuckle; Desert Alchemy essences: Canyon
Grapevine and Spineless Prickly Pear Cactus; Living Essences:
Mauve Melaleuca and Woolly Banksia

Purpose of the mix: Assists you to live in the now, letting go
of the past because you access your optimism to know you are
enough and loved just the way you are.

The Injustice of Injustice Flower Essence Mix: Living
Essences: Blue, Orange, Red, and Yellow Leschenaultia; and
Rose Cone Flower

Purpose of the mix: Assists you in being centred and calm in
all situations and at all times; and enabling you to connect into
your unconditional love, gratitude, and compassion.

notional Freedom Technique

The emotional freedom technique (EFT) was created by Gary Craig, who studied with Dr Roger Callahan, a clinical research psychologist from the United States who was one of the first to develop a technique to clear emotional disturbances from the body using the meridian's energy system. Dr Callahan spent ten years from 1980 to 1990 formulating and testing his technique, thought field therapy. A field of psychology has developed around therapies such as EFT and TFT, and it is called energy psychology.

EFT is one of those rare techniques that can help resolve emotional distress without making a person more upset during the process. Where deeper emotions are accessed, EFT helps them to release easily, allowing a person to stay in control of his or her feelings. It is not only highly effective and extremely easy to do, but it involves little risk of any negative emotional consequences. EFT can be used to de-charge negative emotions, beliefs, memories, and thoughts. It is vital to remember that it only removes the emotional charge, not the meaning or importance or validity of your experience. It is easy to do on one's own and is ideal to be incorporated into one's daily self-care practice.

What does the emotional freedom technique consist of?

It is a simple technique in which specific meridian points are tapped while repeating the issue out loud, to keep the mind focused on what is being released. The issue is initially scored, and then one round of tapping is completed. The issue is then re-scored on how you feel *at that moment*. If required, another round of tapping is completed. Once the issue is at zero, it has been fully de-charged.

The SUDS Scale

It is important to establish the intensity of the emotional charge, and the term used to identify this number is the SUDS level, or subjective units of distress or disturbance. The SUDS score provides the data required to evaluate your progress and ultimately your success in eliminating an issue.

The purpose of the SUDS scale is to gauge some idea of how strongly you feel about the issue being tapped, and to note when that feeling disappears. Traditionally the SUDS scale ranges from zero to ten. Zero means no emotional reaction, and ten is maximum emotional charge. If you prefer to use words like high, medium, low, or zero, then you can.

To obtain a score, simply read the set-up statement, ask what the score is, and listen for a number to pop into your head. Then write it down.

Where are the tapping points?

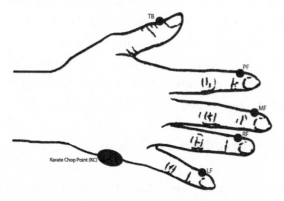

All hand points to be tapped

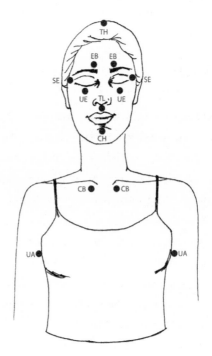

Head and body points to be tapped

The order of tapping is:

Tap the set–up statement on the Karate Chop point. Tap the remainder phrase from the top of the head (TH) in order: eyebrow (EB), side of eye (SE), under the eye (UE), top of lip (TL), chin (CH), under collar bone (CB), under arm (UA), to the hand points of thumb (TB), pointer finger (PF), middle finger (MF), ring finger (RF), and little finger (LF).

Emotional Freedom Technique Process

The wording of EFT looks like this: 'Even though [put the issue here], I deeply and completely accept myself.'

Before you tap your statement, give it a score out of ten. Zero means you don't feel anything about the issue, and ten means it is very stressful. This set-up statement is tapped on the karate chop point and said three times.

Example: '*Even though the more I deny myself, the more I will deny others,* I deeply and completely love and accept myself.'

Then you repeat a reminder phrase (RP) on each of the tapping points, saying it once on each point, which consists of just the issue. Example: '*The more I deny myself, the more I will deny others.*'

You continue tapping until the score is at zero.

Working with EFT and the Injustices

You can either create your own statements or use the words from the description that resonates with you in your set-up statements. Below is a starting point for each injustice. Once you have done a round of tapping, you can write down any thoughts that have come into your consciousness, put those statements into the EFT set-up structure, and then tap them.

Even though fearing that my needs won't be met draws me into the injustice of idleness, I deeply and completely love and accept myself.

RP: Fearing that my needs won't be met draws me into the injustice of idleness.

Even though each time I think I'm acting on my thoughts, words, intentions, and beliefs, but I'm not, I am falling into the injustice of hypocrisy, I deeply and completely love and accept myself.

RP: Each time I think I'm acting on my thoughts, words, intentions, and beliefs, but I'm not, I am falling into the injustice of hypocrisy.

Even though my child's perceptions of love, life, and reality trap me in the injustice of limitations, I deeply and completely love and accept myself.

RP: My child's perceptions of love, life, and reality trap me in the injustice of limitations.

Even though my fear of vulnerability snares me in the injustice of deception, I deeply and completely love and accept myself.

RP: My fear of vulnerability snares me in the injustice of deception.

Even though each time my sense of shame creates suffering in my daily life, it locks me in the injustice of temptation, I deeply and completely love and accept myself.

RP: Each time my sense of shame creates suffering in my daily life, it locks me in the injustice of temptation.

Even though I get lost in my sense of lack when I'm entangled in the injustice of selfishness, I deeply and completely love and accept myself.

RP: I get lost in my sense of lack when I'm entangled in the injustice of selfishness.

Even though each time I get hung up about being perfect, I am consumed in the injustice of vanity, I deeply and completely love and accept myself.

RP: Each time I get hung up about being perfect, I am consumed in the injustice of vanity.

Even though I give my power away when I get hooked into the injustice of intimidation, I deeply and completely love and accept myself.

RP: I give my power away when I get hooked into the injustice of intimidation.

Even though I exert too much power over others when I play into the injustice of intimidation, I deeply and completely love and accept myself.

RP: I exert too much power over others when I play into the injustice of intimidation.

Even though my fears that others will not see, hear, or acknowledge my truth submerges me in the injustice of emotionality, I deeply and completely love and accept myself.

RP: My fear that others will not see, hear, or acknowledge my truth submerges me in the injustice of emotionality.

Even though my sense of insufficiency pulls me into the injustice of injustice, I deeply and completely love and accept myself.

RP: My sense of insufficiency pulls me into the injustice of injustice.

Daily Positive Affirmations

By using daily positive affirmations, you can align yourself with the positive qualities associated with each lesson. You can also use them to pull out any blockages you may have that prevent you from becoming your best self in relation to each injustice.

Ideally, create five positive affirmations to tap once each day for fourteen days. You only tap on the eight points on the head and torso, doing one round for each statement. When creating positive affirmations, always use:

- A time frame like 'now' so that your brain knows when you want to be in the positive state
- Positive active words like choosing, willing, able, becoming or allowing; words like don't, won't, and not focus on the negative and will bring more of what you don't want

Tap each statement only on the head and body points.

Here are some examples of daily positive affirmations for each injustice.

- I am now willing to feel strong in my vulnerability.
- I am now becoming congruent in thought and deed.
- I am now choosing to remember it is my choice how I respond to events in my life.
- I am now choosing to embrace and express my playful, light, and cheeky self.
- I am now allowing myself to stand tall and strong in the presence of others.
- I am now choosing to express my gratitude for all I have and all that is available to me.

- I am now choosing to know deep within myself that I am okay just the way I am.
- I am now maintaining my personal boundaries while allowing others to value and respect me.
- I am now able to be in charge of my real life, the one I am choosing to create every day.
- I am now choosing to positively use my personal power to create whatever I focus on.

Tap Bullies Away App

Bullying in our school yards, workplaces, and homes has become a major issue and relates to the lesson of the injustice of intimidation. Most of the focus is on preventing bullying, but there is very little around to help with the after-effects of being bullied. The App *Tap Bullies Away* is just for that: it helps with recovery from the negative effects of being bullied. Whether someone has been bullied at school, in the workplace, or at home, the app has two emotional freedom technique protocols: one to help you cope with the bullying that has occurred, and the other to help release the distress felt about being bullied. Both should be used to fully clear the experience. The protocols can be used every day or simply when there is a need to build resilience and emotional muscle.

The key is, don't let bullying destroy a life, especially your life or the life of someone you know. This app can make a difference to how you feel. The app is available for iPhone, iPod, and iPad, and it can be purchased through the Apple App Store. The Android version for HTC, Samsung, and Sony Ericsson can be purchased via Google Play.

Matrix Reimprinting

Matrix Reimprinting was created by Karl Dawson and was described by Sasha Allenby in *Matrix Reimprinting Using EFT: Rewrite Your Past, Transform Your Future.* Matrix Reimprinting specifically works with accessing traumatic memories that have spilt off and are being held in the matrix. This memory is called an ECHO. Through the use of EFT tapping, it becomes possible to access the content of the memory by working with the ECHO to release and transform the recollection into a new and productive picture. The trauma collapses, and your interpretations and perceptions shift.

You can find a practitioner to help you process the issues related to the injustices, or alternatively you can learn how to do matrix reimprinting on yourself through one of the many courses run by qualified matrix reimprinting trainers. For more information, go to www.matrixreimprinting.com.

I have created a process to help clear the collective lies we have absorbed during our childhood that create many of our experiences of injustice. It is possible to use the process with traditional EFT on your own, and I will detail that process for you to use or when working with a matrix reimprinting practitioner.

The collective lies consist of our right and perfect messages (RPMs) and how we are judged, condemned, and punished (JCAPs) for being who we are and having our experiences. Some examples of collective lies include:

- Children should be seen but not heard
- Even murderers have mothers who love them
- All women are the same; all men are the same; all black people are the same; all Asians are the same; etc.
- Blood is thicker than water

- You can't have everything you want
- Love makes the world go round; love is all you need
- I'm too dumb; I'm too fat; I'm too skinny; I'm too lazy
- Out of sight out of mind
- The end justifies the means
- Seeing is believing

Clearing the Collective Lie Using EFT

Take a piece of paper and answer the following questions to find the stress or emotional patterns linked into one aspect or experience that you would like to work on from an injustice description. Write down the issue or experience.

Example: Those who are meant to love and want me don't.

What is the collective story or lie?

What do you believe about yourself because of this experience? What thoughts run through your mind about yourself because of this situation? How does this experience click your mind into the collective lie? What stories are run about this situation?

Example: There must be something wrong with me, that I'm bad and unlovable, because even murderers have mothers who love them.

RPMs

How can you be *right* in this situation?

What messages do you have about how you must be right in relation to your issue or experience? Being right means if you do this, then you will be good, right, okay, and worthy.

Example: I need to change my personality to be different, to be less than who I am. I make it impossible for people to love me the way I am.

How can you be *perfect* in this situation?

What messages do you have about how you must be perfect in relation to your issue or experience? Being perfect means if you do this, you will be loved, acceptable, important, and respected.

Example: By being less intense, less deep, and less successful than I am, I will be normal, be like everyone else, or at least be like someone one else in particular.

JCAPs

How do you judge yourself?

In what ways are you not good enough because of this experience? How do you put yourself down? What is your negative, critical self-talk about this situation?

Example: I'm not good enough to receive love, to be wanted, and to be myself.

What don't you deserve because of this experience?

Example: Acceptance, love, and connection.

How do others judge you for this experience?

How do they treat you as if you are not good enough and don't deserve things?

Example: Others withhold their true feelings from me; they hide their vulnerability and blame me for how they feel. I don't deserve to be loved and wanted because I'm strong, already being myself, courageous, empowered, knowledgeable, and insightful—so I don't deserve more.

How do you condemn yourself?

In what ways do you feel bad or ashamed about yourself?

Example: It's not okay to be me. I'm faulty; I expect too much to want to be myself.

How do others condemn you for this experience?

How do others make you feel bad for being you? How do others make you feel ashamed of yourself? What has been said to you that made you feel bad about yourself?

Example: I'm wrong to want others to be open and honest with me, to be all of who they are, and to be their best and most loving selves.

How do you punish yourself?

What do you think you will lose because of this experience? What do you deny yourself as punishment because of this situation?

Example: Peacefulness of connection with others.

How do others punish you?

What will other people take away from you because of this experience? What will other people withhold from you?

Example: Honesty, peace, flow, and joy; instead, it feels hard, difficult, complicated, and joyless.

Now you have the answers, you can tap it all away! Use the tapping order detailed in the section 'Where are the tapping points?'

Go back to your original issue and put it in an EFT set-up statement.

First Round:

Even though *(your issue)*, I deeply and completely accept myself.

Give it a score between—zero and ten.

Score: _____ _____ _____ _____

The reminder phrase is the issue and is tapped on all points.

Reminder phrase: *(what your issue is)*

Example: Even though those who are meant to love and want me don't, I deeply and completely accept myself.

RP: Those who are meant to love and want me don't.

Now, instead of re-scoring you will clear the messages about being right and perfect as well as the judgements, condemnations, and punishments. Then come back to score the original issue. To do these, begin at the top of

the head and tap through the points as laid out below for one round.

Second Round:

Collective Lie: What is the collective story? What have you been told this means about you?

Example: The collective lie I have been told is that there must be something wrong with me, that I'm bad and unlovable if those who are meant to love and want me don't.

Third Round:

Messages about being right:

I can only be right if *(list what you wrote down).*

Example: I can only be right if I change my personality. I need to be different, to be less than who I am. I make it impossible for people to love me by being the way I am.

Fourth Round

Messages about being perfect:

I can only be perfect by *(list what you wrote down).*

Example: I can only be perfect by being less intense, less deep, and less successful; by being less than I am; by being normal; and by being like everyone else (or at least by being someone else in particular).

Fifth Round:

What is your truth about being you?

My soul's truth is that I can only be perfect by *(write a positive statement about yourself)*.

Example: My soul's truth is that I can only be perfect by being myself in all of my depth and intensity, because that is who I am.

Judgement:

Sixth Round:

I feel judged that I'm not good enough *(list what you wrote down)*.

Example: I feel judged that I'm not good enough to receive love, to be wanted, and to be myself.

Seventh Round:

(State your original issue), I feel like I don't deserve *(list what you wrote down)*.

Example: When those who are meant to love and want me don't, I feel like I don't deserve acceptance, love, and connection.

Eighth Round:

I experience others as being *(list what you wrote down)* towards me, and so I feel they are saying I don't deserve *(list what you wrote down)* because *(list what you wrote down)*.

Example: I experience others as withholding their true feelings and vulnerability from me and then blaming me for how they feel, so I feel they are saying I don't deserve to be loved and wanted because I'm strong and already being myself, because I'm courageous, empowered, knowledgeable, and insightful, so I don't deserve more.

Condemnation:

Ninth Round:

I feel condemned that I'm bad for *(list what you wrote down)*

Example: I feel condemned that it's not okay to be me, that I'm faulty, and that I expect too much to want to be myself

Tenth Round:

I experience others as *(list what you wrote down)*.

Example: I experience others as making out that I'm wrong to want them to be open and honest, to be all of who they are, to be their best and most loving selves with me

Punishment:

Eleventh Round:

I feel punished when I lose *(list what you wrote down)*

Example: I feel punished when I lose the peacefulness of connection with others.

Twelfth Round:

I experience others punishing me by withdrawing *(list what you wrote down).*

Example: I experience others punishing me by withdrawing honesty, peace, flow, and joy, but instead making everything feel hard, difficult, complicated, and joyless.

Thirteenth Round:

Positive Affirmations

By now, you should feel ready for some positive statements! Create seven positive statements that describe how you want to feel and be now.

Example: Those who are meant to love and want me don't.

1. *I am now choosing to feel a sense of peace in all my interactions with others.*
2. *I am now willing to connect to my peacefulness at all times and in all situations.*
3. *I am now willing to instantaneously transform all difficulties in communicating with others into peace and love.*
4. *I am now able to feel at peace and completely loved at all times and in all situations.*
5. *I am now choosing to manifest love and peace in all my interactions within myself and others.*
6. *I am now choosing to experience the joy of connection with all there is in each moment.*
7. *I am now choosing to become the breath of peace, love, and joy in union with all there is.*

After tapping the positive affirmations, check your score with the original issue, experience, or fear. When your score is zero, the issue is cleared. If it isn't at zero, tap the statements that still hold a charge until the score reaches zero.

Now It Is Your Choice

This is your life, and you are worth putting in the effort to make your life the best you are capable of. The choice is now yours.

What will you choose to do?

ACKNOWLEDGEMENTS

THIS HAS BEEN AN AMAZING journey from the first flashes of insight to the formulation of a book that bought together many ideas into a whole story to share with others. My biggest expression of gratitude and thanks is to my father, Stuart Murray; without you as my father, influencing everything about my life, this book would never even been conceived. To my friends, for all their support and encouragement; I am indebted to you. To Gianna Sponchiado; thank you for all of your editing advice. To Sylvia Dardha; thank you for your support, involvement in the workshops, and the amazing work you and Michael Christian did with the crowd funding project to help get this book out into the world, as well as this beautiful book cover.

Thank you to everyone who has directly contributed to the insights of injustice, enabling me to write them in such a way that they can resonate with others. To every person I've ever met, observed, or listened to stories about: you have all contributed to the awareness of the role injustice plays in our life, especially Marion Monk, Perianne Tassell, Melinda Albers, Sue North, Dick Cohen, Ross Lyons, Gianna Sponchiado, Leigh Burrage, Barbara White, Kellie Beverly, Gillian Gavin, Brooke Lambeth, Heather Hastings, Darryl Blackwell, Rebecca

Reberger, Kerri Mackay, Amanda Walsh, Erin Richardson, and Sylvia Dardha.

To Peter Laidlaw; you know why you are here!

I was incredibly grateful for the opportunity to present my book to Hay House after attending the Writer's Workshop held in Sydney in August 2012. Thank you to the Balboa Press publishing team for helping me to bring this book to the world.

ABOUT THE AUTHOR

LEONIE BLACKWELL HAS BEEN RUNNING her naturopathic business, The Essence of Healing, in Drouin since 1994. She has worked with flower essences in a school setting, in a youth refuge, and with clients for over twenty-three years, and she has been using EFT in her practice since 2001. She provides accredited practitioner training and innovative personal development seminars and workshops. The flower essence course is the longest running course in Australia at eighteen years, and the emotional freedom technique was the first and only course meeting Australian educational standards; it was created in 2007. Leonie has provided health guidance to over two thousand clients and has taught hundreds through personal development workshops, professional development seminars, and practitioner training. The Essence of Healing was a finalist in the Gippsland Business Awards 2012.

Leonie has created a world-first app, Tap Bullies Away, condensing her vast experience of EFT into a simple, creative, and innovative tool to facilitate the recovery of those who have experienced bullying.

For further information, visit www.leonieblackwell.com
Follow Leonie on Twitter: www.twitter.com\leonieblackwell
Follow Leonie on Facebook: www.facebook.com\
makingsenseoftheinsensible

CPSIA information can be obtained
at www.ICGtesting.com
Printed in the USA
BVOW06s2132070218
507582BV00001B/21/P